# LABRADOR RETRIEVER

TERRY ALBERT

## Labrador Retriever

Editor: Stephanie Fornino
Copy Editor: Joann Woy
Indexer: Elizabeth Walker
Series Designer: Mary Ann Kahn
Book Designer: Angela Stanford

TFH Publications®
President/CEO: Glen S. Axelrod
Executive Vice President: Mark E. Johnson
Publisher: Christopher T. Reggio
Production Manager: Kathy Bontz

TFH Publications, Inc.
One TFH Plaza
Third and Union Avenues
Neptune City, NJ 07753

Discovery Communications, Inc. Book Development Team: Marjorie Kaplan, President and General Manager, Animal Planet Media / Kelly Day, EVP and General Manager, Discovery Commerce / Elizabeth Bakacs, Vice President, Licensing and Creative / JP Stoops, Director, Licensing / Bridget Stoyko, Associate Art Director

Printed and bound in China

11 12 13 14 15 16   1 3 5 7 9 8 6 4 2

Library of Congress Cataloging-in-Publication Data
Albert, Terry, 1951-
  Labrador retriever / Terry Albert.
    p. cm.
  Includes index.
  ISBN 978-0-7938-3718-2 (alk. paper)
  1.  Labrador retriever.  I. Title.
  SF429.L3A43 2011
  636.752'7--dc22
                    2010052558

This book has been published with the intent to provide accurate and authoritative information in regard to the subject matter within. While every reasonable precaution has been taken in preparation of this book, the author and publisher expressly disclaim responsibility for any errors, omissions, or adverse effects arising from the use or application of the information contained herein. The techniques and suggestions are used at the reader's discretion and are not to be considered a substitute for veterinary care. If you suspect a medical problem consult your veterinarian.

Note: In the interest of concise writing, "he" is used when referring to puppies and dogs unless the text is specifically referring to females or males. "She" is used when referring to people. However, the information contained herein is equally applicable to both sexes.

*The Leader In Responsible Animal Care for Over 50 Years!*®
**www.tfh.com**

# CONTENTS

# ORIGINS OF YOUR
# LABRADOR RETRIEVER

The Labrador Retriever is truly a dog for all reasons, whether he is a show dog, service dog, hunting partner, or family pet. A relative newcomer compared to other breeds, Labs were developed to be working companions capable of enduring harsh conditions without complaint, all while enthusiastically performing the many jobs they were and are asked to do.

So how did our "wash-and-wear" canine companion become such a versatile and friendly dog? To understand the Labrador Retriever of today, let's look back to the beginning of man's relationship with dogs and the development of the breed.

## THE DEVELOPMENT OF THE DOG

Sometime in our ancient past, between 15,000 and 20,000 years ago, man and wolf formed a bond that would affect the survival and evolution of both species. Humans were still nomadic, not yet raising their own food animals or crops. As they migrated across Asia, the gray wolf, a scavenger who ate the leftover bones and waste that man left behind, followed them. The nomads appreciated their new traveling companions because the wolves, with their acute senses of smell and hearing, alerted them to nearby predators and game that they then killed for food.

The two lived side by side, each benefiting from the other's presence. Some wolves were probably eaten, but those who were the least threatening or fearful had litters of pups that grew up accepting their human neighbors. Over generations, the wolf's partnership with its human benefactors led to cooperative tracking, hunting, and guarding ventures.

As the nomadic tribes reached Africa and Europe, they brought their dogs with them, possibly also domesticating native wolf populations along the way. When the agricultural revolution began about 10,000 years ago, civilization evolved from hunting and gathering to more permanent settlements and agricultural communities. By this time, man was specifically breeding those wolves/dogs who were least aggressive and had other desirable characteristics. Dogs became herders, draft animals, livestock guardians, and companions—in other words: domesticated.

## THE ST. JOHN'S DOG IN NEWFOUNDLAND

Although dogs first arrived in North America from the west, via the Bering Strait between Russia and Alaska, it is believed that the first dogs to arrive on the eastern shore of Canada didn't reach the area until the early 16th century. At this time, wealthy ship owners from Britain, Portugal, and France began sending

Labs were developed to be working companions capable of enduring harsh conditions without complaint.

their ships to the shores of the Avalon Peninsula, at the southeastern tip of Newfoundland, where they fished the abundant waters from spring through fall of each year.

The fishermen on these schooners brought along their "water dogges," an ancestor of the retriever breeds, and possibly the St. Hubert's Hound, a breed that also contributed to the development of the Bloodhound. The exact origins of the Labrador Retriever are uncertain, as no written records were kept. However, over the next two centuries, the fishermen worked side by side with their dogs in the harsh icy climate, and it is believed that the breed that would ultimately become the Labrador was developed. That dog was called the St. John's Dog, after the fishing village the English established along the southeastern coast.

The St. John's Dog was also known as the Lesser Newfoundland, in order to differentiate it from the Greater Newfoundland found in other parts of the country. The larger draft dog with the heavy coat became the Newfoundland dog we know today. Historians debate about which of the two breeds came first and if they were interbred. There are excellent arguments on both sides. Some speculate that Portuguese Mastiffs were bred with the St. John's Dog to produce the Greater Newfoundland. Others believe that the large black draft dog was bred with smaller spaniels and retrievers to produce the Lesser Newfoundland.

St. John's Dogs were strong swimmers and small enough for a fisherman to take out in his dory, a small, shallow boat. These utilitarian canines pulled in nets and retrieved fish that had escaped from the hooks. The dogs had webbed feet, a sword-like tail that steered them well in the water, and a short, water-repellent double coat. These traits, coupled with their excellent disposition, soft mouth, and hunting ability, also helped the St. John's Dog excel at retrieving shot game on land and in water.

## THE LABRADOR RETRIEVER IN BRITAIN

Trade between Newfoundland and England was brisk, and by the 1700s the Newfoundlanders were taking their dogs with them to Poole Harbour, the main port used for commerce between England and Newfoundland. The English were impressed by this small working dog and realized the advantage of having a dog who could retrieve on both land and in water.

By 1835, the English were actively importing the breed to use for hunting on their estates, and they referred to them as Labrador dogs.

Before the retrieving breeds were developed, British gentlemen hunted with pointers and setters. When the St. John's Dog arrived in England, some kennels began to breed the dogs to retrieving setters, pointers, and possibly even some foxhounds. To their credit, their goal was to develop a better hunting dog, and they were not distracted by fads or fashion. Some attribute this early interbreeding with the differences in body "style" we still see in Labradors today.

## THE LAB'S RISE IN POPULARITY IN ENGLAND

No one knows for sure how or when the breed's name changed to Labrador, but one theory is that the Portuguese fishermen who populated Newfoundland used their word "lavrador," meaning "laborer." Others suspect that some in Britain confused Newfoundland with Labrador, an area to the north. Whatever the origin, by 1835, the English were actively importing the dogs to use for hunting on their estates, and they referred to them as Labrador dogs.

Two families are recognized as being the first to develop the Lab by importing and breeding St. John's Dogs in Britain. The fifth and sixth Dukes of Buccleuch, in Scotland, and the first and second Earl of Malmesbury, in England, worked together to breed dogs for their own use while keeping the Labrador true to his origins. The third Earl of Malmesbury continued to develop the breed as its popularity as a shooting dog spread.

The practice of importing dogs ended abruptly in 1885, for two reasons. Newfoundland enacted the Sheep Protection Act, which imposed a duty, or tax, on dogs, so that the canine population immediately began to diminish, and ultimately, the St. John's Dog disappeared. At the same time, England imposed a strict quarantine on imported dogs. The two laws, in effect, made it almost impossible to import or export any dogs.

It was up to Britain to ensure the breed's future, and the country did an admirable job of it. By the late 1800s, the versatile Labrador dog was considered a necessity for hunting, and breeders at major estates and kennels were breeding to establish "type," the characteristics that make a Lab recognizable as a Lab.

### KENNEL CLUB RECOGNITION

In 1903, the Labrador Retriever was recognized and accepted in the (British) Kennel Club stud book, and the first championship in the breed's history was awarded in 1906, to Broome Park Bob, owned and bred by Lord Knutsford.

### THE LABRADOR RETRIEVER CLUB

It wasn't until 1916 that the Labrador Retriever Club in England was founded and a breed standard was formally written and approved.

It wasn't until 1917 that the American Kennel Club (AKC) recognized the Labrador Retriever as its own breed.

### THE LABRADOR RETRIEVER IN AMERICA

The Annual New York Dog Show of 1885 (later known as the Westminster Kennel Club Show) lists the "English Retriever" (yet another name for the Labrador) in its entries. The new breed was slow to catch on in the United States. James Watson, in his 1906 *The Dog Book*, wrote that the American style of shooting was different from

In addition to the national parent club, more than 45 regional breed clubs and hunting retriever organizations in the United States work to preserve the Lab's original purpose.

the English. British shooters did not want their setters or pointers touching the dead game, and they therefore used retrievers for that purpose. The Americans preferred setters or pointers who would also retrieve, so they had no need to add another dog. Watson's book profiles only the Chesapeake and Curly-Coated Retrievers because he felt the Lab would never catch on in the States.

## AMERICAN KENNEL CLUB (AKC) RECOGNITION

At this time in history, Labrador, Curly-Coated, Flat-Coated, Chesapeake Bay, and Golden Retrievers were all shown in the same class at a dog show. Depending on a dog's characteristics, some dogs from the same litter would be listed as two different "breeds" at the same show. It wasn't until 1917 that the American Kennel Club (AKC) recognized the Labrador Retriever as a separate breed.

## THE LAB'S RISE IN POPULARITY IN THE US

In the 1920s, wealthy sportsmen in the eastern United States, used to hunting with Labs in Scotland and Britain, began importing Labradors in greater numbers. They also brought over Scottish trainers and began holding field trials among themselves. Owning Labrador Retrievers became a status symbol. The Lab quickly overtook other retrieving breeds in popularity, and breeding began in earnest in the United States.

All this glamour ended with the Great Depression and World Wars I and II. The wealthy landowners and grand estates became scarce; money was tight, and opulent living was out of fashion. Some kennels were closed down and the dogs dispersed. After the wars, in a new era of prosperity, Middle America began to appreciate, and hunt, with the Labrador. Now the station wagon set began to compete side by side with high society at field trials and dog shows, and the Lab's sunny personality transformed him into America's favorite family pet, as well as a hunting companion.

## LABRADOR RETRIEVER BREED CLUBS

The American parent club, the Labrador Retriever Club, Inc. (LRC), was formed in 1931, and in December of that same year, the AKC held its first retriever field trial. The first Labrador national specialty show was held in May of 1933 and was judged by Mrs. Marshall Field, president of the parent club. The Best in Show winner was Boli of Blake, who also became the first Labrador to earn the American Champion title on November 1, 1933, in New York City.

In addition to the national parent club, today more than 45 regional breed clubs and numerous hunting retriever organizations throughout the United States actively promote Labs and work to preserve their original purpose.

Breed clubs do more than just hold dog shows and hand out ribbons to pretty dogs. They are active in all aspects of their breed. Some of the activities that the LRC supports are:
• participating in conformation, obedience, agility competitions, and other companion dog events
• engaging in working certificate tests, hunting tests, and field trials to maintain the breed as a working retriever
• awarding conformation certificates to encourage better breeding
• supporting Labrador Retriever health research
• providing referrals to breeders
• maintaining the breed standard
• publishing a code of ethics for those who breed and show
• educating the public on health, training, and all aspects of the breed
• encouraging and supporting junior showmanship
• supporting breed rescue for homeless Labradors
• collecting and preserving the history of the breed
• supporting legislation that benefits dogs and their owners

The LRC website is www.thelabradorclub.com. Contact information for AKC regional breed clubs is available at www.akc.org.

In addition to the LRC, in 1996 the National Labrador Retriever Club (NLRC) was formed to promote the betterment of the breed and encourage more pet owners to actively join in Labrador activities. This club, not affiliated with the AKC, promotes a different breed standard, one used by the Fédération Cynologique Internationale (FCI), also known as the World Canine Organization (WCO). Eighty countries throughout the world participate but not the United States. For more information, visit its website at www.nationallabradorretrieverclub.com.

Breed clubs, like the Labrador Retriever Club, Inc., are active in all aspects of their breed.

Fanciers who are interested in hunting tests and field trials also earn titles through the North American Hunting Retriever Association (NAHRA). They were originally a part of the AKC, and the two clubs worked together to develop a joint hunting test for retrievers. Now separate organizations, supported clubs are located throughout the United States and Canada. Visit the NAHRA's website at www.nahra.org.

In 1991, the AKC held the first Master National Hunting Test for Retrievers. Fifty-nine clubs joined forces to promote the breeding and training of retriever breeds and founded the Master National Retriever Club (MNRC). There are now more than 150 member clubs, and the MNRC still conducts the annual Master National Stake. The website is www.masternational.com.

## LABRADOR COLORS

The earliest litters of both the greater and lesser Newfoundland had liver (now called chocolate) and occasionally yellow puppies, but these were usually considered undesirable.

### THE ORIGIN OF BLACK LABRADORS

Because black was genetically dominant and therefore appeared most often, it was established as the preferred color. Early St. John's Dogs had a white splash on the chest and white feet. This gradually disappeared, and a solid black dog became the norm. Today, a small white spot on the chest is still permissible but not favored in the show ring.

## THE ORIGIN OF CHOCOLATE LABRADORS

Chocolate is carried in a recessive gene, and a few chocolate dogs were brought back to England from the very beginning. In 1807, a shipwreck off the Maryland coast left two St. John's Dogs in America who were originally bound for the third Earl of Malmesbury in England. They became the foundation dogs for the Chesapeake Bay Retriever, and one was a "dingy red," or liver.

We first hear about chocolates in Britain, in 1892, when Lord Dalkeith reported two "livers" being whelped at his Buccleuch kennel in Scotland. At the first field trial held in England, in 1900, the winner was a "wavy coated liver bitch" named Abbott's Rust. Chocolates were well on their way to acceptance by the early years of the new century, but it wasn't until 1956 that a chocolate dog became an American champion, and 1964 before there was a chocolate English champion.

## THE ORIGIN OF YELLOW LABRADORS

Long before breeding records were kept in either Newfoundland or England, yellow dogs occasionally appeared in some gundog breeds. Like the chocolates, yellows were originally culled because the color was considered a fault. The first recorded yellow Lab was Ben of Hyde, born in 1899, in England, from two

Labs come in three colors: black (left), yellow (middle), and chocolate (right).

For the past two decades, Labs have been the most popular breed in both the United States and Britain.

black Labradors who had been imported from Newfoundland. His owner, Major Radclyffe, and a few close associates began breeding for the color. Ben produced many yellow puppies.

By 1910, more breeders were trying to specifically produce yellow Labs, but as they bred for color, other characteristics began to suffer; yellows often had long spindly legs or houndy ears. To address this problem and get consistency within the breed, an English club called the Yellow Labrador Club was established with its own breed standard. This new club served its purpose but was eventually disbanded, although yellows remained a part of the Labrador breed, judged by the same standard as blacks and chocolates. In 1913 the first yellow Lab was shown in England, although judges still preferred black to yellow at that time. One fancier in the late 1920s who entered her yellow Lab was turned away at ringside and told to take her dog to the Golden Retriever ring.

The 1920s to 1930s saw the yellow Lab's popularity grow, and as American breeders imported stud dogs from England, more yellows began to appear in the US. The first Labrador to win a field trial in the United States was an imported yellow, Carl of Boghurst. After World War II, their popularity surged, and by the 1950s yellow was completely assimilated into the breed in both countries. Entries of yellows were often equal to or outnumbered black and chocolate Labradors at dog shows, and this is still true today.

## LABRADOR RETRIEVERS TODAY

For the past two decades, Labs have been the most popular breed in both the United States and Britain, with more than double the number registered than the next closest breed. Labs are still popular as hunting dogs, and their drive, companionability, and intelligence have also made them a popular working dog in other arenas. Labradors serve as assistance dogs for the disabled, therapy dogs, arson and bomb detectors, search-and-rescue dogs, police dogs, and more.

And we can't forget their most important role: family pet. Everywhere you go, you see people with their Labs: dog park, beach, walking, jogging, and picnicking. Labs also love children, and when taught to be gentle with each other, the two often form a lifelong bond.

This popularity has caused some problems, leading to an overabundance of poorly bred Labradors who have overly hyper temperaments, are too big, and have inherited orthopedic and other health problems. Unscrupulous individuals produce litters without regard for the betterment of the breed, and their unsound puppies end up in the homes of unsuspecting families. It is the dogs who suffer, and many are surrendered to shelters. Labrador rescue groups rehabilitate and rehome thousands of dogs every year.

The good news is that many responsible breeders do exist, and they are working to eliminate health problems while they preserve and improve the breed. These breeders put on dog shows, field trials, and hunting tests nationwide to showcase the Labrador's beauty, talent, and retrieving ability.

Over several centuries, the Labrador Retriever has developed into a superb hunting dog and loyal family companion, and breed clubs are striving to preserve the best characteristics of the breed. Now, let's look closer at the 21st-century Labrador and how he fits into our households.

# CHARACTERISTICS
# OF YOUR
# LABRADOR RETRIEVER

**A**s the Labrador Retriever has transitioned from fishing to hunting to show dog to family companion, his physical attributes have not changed much from those of the original retriever who pulled in fish on the shores of Newfoundland so many years ago. His happy-go-lucky personality, trainability, and intelligence have also been documented throughout the breed's history.

## PHYSICAL CHARACTERISTICS

The Labrador is built for work without being too big, too small, or too fussy-looking; he's your basic wash-and-wear all-purpose dog.

### OVERALL DESCRIPTION

A Lab is a medium-sized, strongly built, active family dog. Developed as a retrieving gundog to fetch waterfowl and upland game, the Labrador has tremendous endurance, coupled with the desire to spend long hours at his owner's side, whether that owner is pheasant hunting or watching television by the fireplace.

### BODY

I would describe a Lab's body as a log on four posts: very slight tapering from front to back, a round chest, sturdy legs, and a round thick "branch" of a tail. Labs are just a bit longer than they are tall at the shoulders—not quite a square profile. The thick but graceful neck supports a chiseled, distinctive head. When compared to the fine bones and slim bodies of some of his sporting cousins, like pointers and setters, you'll realize there's nothing dainty about a Labrador. This sturdy body serves him well when he's asked to spend long hours running through the underbrush retrieving game.

A Lab is a medium-sized, strongly built, active family dog.

### Tail

One of the most distinctive features of the Labrador Retriever is his tail. Described as an "otter tail," it is carried straight back and is wide at the base, gradually tapering a bit at the end. A Lab occasionally has a gay tail, meaning it is carried up in the air, but it should never curl up over his back. Covered with his distinctive thick double coat, the tail is of medium length and sometimes has a "twizzle" of crooked hairs at the end.

### Ears

A Labrador's ears are very distinctive and provide a quick way to tell if a dog is a mixed breed. The ears hang down in an upside-down triangle shape and lay flat against his cheeks. You should be able to pull the ear forward to completely cover the eye on the same side as the ear. Lab mixes often have "airplane ears" that stick out to the side or are upright at the base.

**BE AWARE!**

Although Labs are almost universally friendly toward other dogs, if you are going to get two dogs, get either one of each sex or two males. Two females, especially if they are related, are the least likely to get along. And it is never a good idea to get littermates. Siblings become more attached to each other than to their people, and because their temperaments might be so evenly matched, they are more likely to squabble.

### Feet

Harking back to their days as a water dog, Labs have webbed feet, a trait they hold in common with other breeds known for swimming, such as the Newfoundland and Portuguese Water Dog.

### Eyes and Expression

You can't talk about the Labrador character without mentioning his kindly eyes and soft expression. They give you a look that melts your heart, and their good nature is evident to everyone they encounter.

Some Labs have a "zipper," or ridge of upright hair, down the middle of their foreheads between the eyes.

### SIZE

The size and build of a Lab varies greatly from dog to dog. Males should be between 22½ to 24½ inches (57.2 to 62.2 cm) at the withers (shoulders) and 65 to 80 pounds (29.5 to 36.3 kg). Females range from 21½ to 23½ inches (54.6 to 60 cm) and 55 to 70 pounds (25 to 31.8 kg). This describes the "ideal" Labrador set forth in the breed standard by the American Kennel Club (AKC), and show dogs must conform to this standard. In reality, most pet Labs tend to be at the tall end of the spectrum, with a few as tall as 27 inches (68.6 cm) and weighing more than 100 pounds (45.4 kg).

Lab fanciers refer to so-called "English," or "show-type" Labradors versus "American" or "field type." If you visit a dog show, you'll see shorter, stockier Labs, often with a mellower temperament. "Field-bred" dogs are usually taller, leaner, more high strung, and more energetic than their stocky counterparts, and they're not usually seen in the show ring. On the other hand, many show-type Labs compete in hunting events and obtain performance titles, proving that, although there is great variation in the breed, both types can still do the job they were originally bred to do.

"Field-bred" dogs are usually taller, leaner, more high strung, and more energetic than their stocky counterparts, and they're not usually seen in the show ring.

Since the early days of the 20th century, a philosophical split has existed between field and show breeders, with both sides worried that the original Labrador would be lost forever. In the 1990s, a group of fanciers filed a lawsuit objecting to revisions in the standard that required dogs to fall within certain height limitations. The suit was ultimately dismissed, and the revised standard became effective in February 1994.

## COAT

The Labrador coat is short and dense, not smooth or soft. The double coat features a harsh outercoat made up of water and dirt-repellent guard hairs and a softer undercoat that provides insulation from cold and harsh weather. The coat may have a slight wave over the shoulders, where it is longer and thicker. Even the tail has a thick covering of fur. The undercoat sheds heavily every spring.

## COLORS

The original Labradors were black, which is the genetically dominant color and most common. Yellow and chocolate Labs were not as common but are very popular today. All three colors can appear in the same litter, depending on the genetic makeup of the parents. In all three colors, a small white spot, no bigger than a silver dollar, is allowable on the chest, a reminder of the original St. John's Dog.

## Black Labs

A black Lab should have dark brown eyes and black pigment on his nose and around his mouth and eye rims. Black or yellow eyes are not correct but of course have no effect on the dog's ability to be an excellent pet.

## Yellow Labs

Yellow Labradors range from a light cream to a dark fox red. Lighter dogs may have some tan shading on the ears and over the shoulders, but it should not appear patchy. So-called white Labradors are really a very light yellow, so pale that they appear white. Beware of breeders who want to charge more for the "rare" fox red Labrador. This is just a dark yellow dog. Yellow Labs have brown or hazel eyes, with brown being preferred.

The term "golden Lab" is incorrect. There are Golden Retrievers and Labrador Retrievers, and a golden Lab would be a mix of the two breeds. In the late 19th century, yellow Labs in England were commonly a darker tone than you see today, and that is probably where the "golden" term originated.

Yellow Labs should have black pigmentation around the mouth, eyes, and on the nose. A "Dudley" yellow Lab has pink or chocolate pigmentation, which is incorrect for the show ring but perfectly acceptable for a companion dog. Some yellows exhibit

what is called "snow nose," in which the black nose fades to pink or a mottled combination of black and pink. This is not a defect and has no effect on the dog's health or ability to smell.

Yellow Labradors range from a light cream to a dark fox red, pictured here.

## Chocolate Labs

Chocolate Labradors are seen in various shades from light brown to deep chocolate, so dark that it is sometimes mistaken for black at first glance. The eyes range from dark brown to yellow. The pigmentation around the eyes, mouth, and nose is also supposed to be chocolate, ranging from pink (not preferred) to deep brown.

There is a popular myth that chocolate Labs are more hyperactive and harder to train. No genetic link

What will your puppy look like as an adult? By looking at the parents and comparing puppies to each other, you'll have a rough idea of what body "type" your Labrador will have when he grows up. When comparing littermates, some are lanky and some are stocky little bulldozers. Yellow puppies don't get noticeably darker or lighter as they mature.

between behavior and color has been established. A dog bred from hunting lines is much more likely to be a wild child, no matter what color he is. Author William Gordon Stables wrote in *Our Friend, the Dog*, in 1903: "...the Livers should in every respect be the same as the Blacks (in) that they are excellent water dogs and are even more lively than the Black retrievers and are more easily excited." Could this be the origin of the claim that chocolate Labs are more hyper? No one knows for sure.

## Silver Labs?

You may see advertisements for "silver" Labrador Retrievers. These dogs are one of two things: either a genetically diluted chocolate or a mix with a Weimaraner, a gray sporting dog.

## Mismarked Labradors

Occasionally, a puppy is born with tan "points"—markings over the eyes and on the chest and legs. This is a throwback to the Gordon Setters who were bred to Labs in England during the early years of the breed. A "splash" puppy is another occasional surprise in an otherwise normal litter. This genetic mix-up results in a dog with patches of another color, ranging anywhere from the tiniest speck of black on a yellow dog to large splashes of yellow on a black or chocolate dog. Another variation: brindle markings (dark broken stripes on a brown background), which appear very rarely, on the legs and chest of a black dog.

Again, any purebred Labrador, whether "correct," "preferred," or totally mismarked, makes a great pet and hunting dog. He just isn't eligible to show in conformation at an AKC dog show. These Labs are, however, eligible to compete in performance events as long as they are spayed or neutered. Dogs who do not conform to the breed standard are not more valuable, so don't fall for scams from disreputable breeders.

# LIVING WITH A LABRADOR RETRIEVER

This fun-loving breed is known for its consistent temperament: easygoing and adaptable to almost any family situation.

## COMPANIONABILITY

One reason Labs are so popular is that they get along with virtually everyone. From the moment you meet, you'll be friends for life, especially if you have a treat in your pocket.

### Labs and Children

Whether telling secrets out in the backyard clubhouse or catching tadpoles in the creek, there is something magical about the bond between a child and a dog. The ultimate buddy, a Lab happily tolerates a lot of tugs and hugs from kids. Because of their size, Labradors sometimes play too roughly for toddlers, but as long as their interactions are supervised, the two can become lifelong friends. Labby is always ready to serve as a pillow or lend a sympathetic ear when times get tough.

Teach your kids how to behave around dogs so that they'll be safe. When the dog and kids get too excited, call a time-out and put Labby in his crate for a break. If the

The ultimate buddy, a Lab happily tolerates a lot of attention from kids.

dog starts jumping or nipping at the children, show them how to stand still and hold their arms close to their sides. If they wave their arms around and yell (like most kids do), the dog will think that they are playing. Even a well-mannered Lab has his limits. If a child hits or pinches too hard, the dog will discipline her in the only way he knows how: with his teeth. And it's the dog who usually suffers for this mistake, ending up euthanized for acting like a dog.

### Labs and Other Pets

Labs are generally friendly with other dogs of all breeds and love to play. A poorly socialized dog might take a while to warm up, but he'll usually come around a lot faster than less

Labs are generally friendly with other dogs of all breeds, and they love to play.

sociable breeds. Introduce new dogs to each other on neutral territory; meet at a park or take them for a walk together.

Most dogs love to chase cats, probably because cats run first and make friends later. But if introduced quietly in a controlled situation, many Labs live peacefully and even become great friends with kitties in the household. To introduce the two, tie the dog to the couch leg or put him in a crate and let the cat come out on his own when he is ready, which usually takes a day or two. Also, let them get used to each other's smell on either side of a closed door. Finally, introduce your Lab on leash so that the chase stops before it begins, and provide a safe place for Kitty to escape. No matter how well your Lab gets along with your cat, he'll still give chase to any invading cats who dare to venture into your yard.

A Lab has a soft mouth because he needs to return the retrieved bird to the hunter without mauling it. But don't assume that he won't chomp the parakeet or flatten the hamster with a hefty paw. They can be friends, but sometimes Labs play pretty roughly, so birds and pocket pets are probably safer in their cages.

## ENVIRONMENT

Labs are so adaptable and people oriented that they settle in quickly if rehomed and live happily almost anywhere, from the country to the suburbs. An apartment or condo is not the ideal home for a Labrador, although you can certainly make it work if you provide training and regular exercise. You don't have to have a big yard because dogs usually lie around all day while you are at work. A 5- or 6-foot (1.5- or 2-m) fence contains most Labs, but there is always the exception. An athletic (or bored) dog will find a foothold and be over it in a flash.

Labs are not meant to be an outside-only or kennel dog—they are happiest when indoors or outdoors with you, doing whatever you are doing, going wherever you are going. A Lab who is left outside all the time is likely to develop problem behaviors like barking, digging, and chewing.

## EXERCISE

His history as a gundog is partly why a Lab makes such a good family pet. When used for duck hunting, he must sit quietly at the hunter's side for long hours, waiting for the command to retrieve a downed bird. Then he gets a short burst of strenuous exercise as he plunges into the water or runs over the fields and retrieves the duck. He finally returns to the hunter's side for another long period of quiet until the next bird is shot. This means, as long he also gets several sessions of play and exercise each day, your Lab is happy to spend long hours in the house lying quietly at your feet.

Labs love to retrieve, and yours will burn off some of that energy he has stored up if you throw a tennis ball or bumper for him. Outings to the dog park, competitive dog sports, and training sessions will exercise his mind as well as his body. A quick walk around the block is not enough exercise for a Lab.

## INTELLIGENCE

The Labrador's sense of humor will keep you constantly entertained, even when some of his antics challenge your patience. Thinkers and problem solvers, they are so smart that they sometimes make up their own games, with you as the helpless participant. Here are some examples:

Duffy, my foster black Lab, hadn't quite figured out the pool at my house, so when I tossed a tennis ball into the water, he stood with his head cocked to one side, trying to figure out how to get to the ball. Finally he bent over edge of the pool and pawed the water, making waves that brought the ball back to the edge of the pool. Triumphant, he fetched it up and brought it to me. This dog was far too smart to be a mere pet; he'd drive his new owner crazy. He was placed with law enforcement in Los Angeles as a bomb-sniffing dog.

My friend Virginia's first foster dog, Snickers, initiated her into rescue on his first day in her home. She left him indoors with her yellow Lab, Siegfried, and went to work. She got a call at work a few hours later. "There's a dog on your roof," said the neighbor. "What color?" she asked. "Chocolate," replied the neighbor. She headed home to rescue her new charge, who had broken a screen and climbed out an upstairs window.

On a similar note: Bud, a yellow Lab, was so well housetrained that he couldn't bear to have an accident in the house. So he broke out an upstairs window screen, went out on the deck to relieve himself, and then came back in and napped until his owner returned.

I used to worry about Indy, another foster dog, when he went out to the barn with me. Our donkey, Bandit, didn't like dogs and would chase them. Indy thought it was great fun. He'd run across the 2-acre pasture with Bandit hot on his heels, a big wide Labrador grin on his face. One day, he suddenly reversed directions and chased Bandit, who bucked and hee-hawed and took off. Indy stayed a respectful distance behind, and they changed places several times, enjoying the game. They never touched each other.

## MALE AND FEMALE TEMPERAMENT

Males and females have similar temperaments once they are spayed or neutered. Females tend to be more independent, napping in the next room rather than at your feet. Males tend to be more bonded with their owners—they are real "Velcro dogs."

## TRAINABILITY

Because they are so versatile, good-natured, and trainable, generations of Labradors have worked as service dogs, in arson and drug detection, bomb sniffing, search and rescue, and a host of other jobs. Enthusiastic and food motivated, they are one of the easiest breeds to train. And train you must. Without training, they make their own fun, and it probably won't be a game you appreciate. A rambunctious, untrained adult Lab is hard to control and harder to train, so start training the minute your new dog or puppy comes home.

Whether or not you are actively training him, your Lab is observing and learning the rules of the world around him. Don't confine training to structured sessions. Dogs, especially Labs, are so in tune to people and their body language that they constantly read signals and evaluate what they mean. It won't take yours long to figure out what he can get away with. He'll also test you to be sure that you really mean it when you give a command, so a firm, not harsh, hand is occasionally necessary.

Labs don't mind repetitive exercises as long as you make the lessons interesting. Reward him with toys and games of fetch, and you'll have an enthusiastic partner

# Dog Tale

In the Northwest, winter days end early; by 3:30 p.m. dusk is settling in, and by 4:30 p.m. it is pitch black outside. My evening routine with the horses always included my Lab Tank. He would busy himself investigating smells while I doled out the hay, changed water, and picked up manure in the stalls.

Because we were hoping to compete in obedience in the spring, sometimes we'd run through a few exercises when I finished the horse chores: a couple of retrieves, a *drop-on recall*, and maybe send him over a jump I had set up in the barn for the winter.

This particular night, Tank sailed over the jump and came to a screeching stop facing the closed barn door. My happy-go-lucky Lab turned into Cujo, hackles up and a low growl rumbling in his throat. He crept forward, body low and tense. I moved behind him and waited.

Suddenly, the barn door opened and in walked my husband. Tank immediately turned puppy happy, wiggling his butt in ecstasy as he ran to say hello.

I've always been told a Lab will welcome a burglar to the house, show him the family jewels, and then ask for a treat. Not on this night. My hero dog was there to protect me when the bogeyman was out in the night.

who loves learning new things. Labs are intensely focused on their work, a tribute to their hunting origins, where they exhibited single-minded dedication to retrieving.

Labrador rescue volunteers report the most common reason why owners relinquish their dogs: They didn't know what they were getting into when they got a Lab. Young, enthusiastic, untrained Labs come into rescue and shelters far too often. These dogs, starved for attention and structure in their lives, are usually successfully rehabbed and placed in permanent homes where they thrive. It's a tribute to the breed that a Lab of any age, with training and discipline, can transition from wild child to perfect pet.

## WATCHDOG ABILITY

Labs are not guard dogs, although they definitely tell you when someone pulls in the driveway or something is going on that worries them. Once he stops alarm barking, a Lab is more likely to lick the intruder to death rather than attack. In fact, because of his strong instinct to retrieve and carry, your Lab will probably greet guests with his favorite stuffed animal or some other treasured toy in his mouth.

# SUPPLIES FOR YOUR
# LABRADOR RETRIEVER

**W**hen I think of supplies for a Lab, the first requirements I think of are "washable" and "chew-proof." Whether you have a puppy or an adult, you'll find that age doesn't matter in the dirt and destruction game. Save yourself some money—buy easy-care, indestructible items.

You don't need a lot of fancy supplies to keep your dog healthy and safe. Unless you have a very large Lab, he doesn't require the biggest size of everything to keep him comfortable. A Labrador Retriever is meant to be a medium-sized dog, but I often see owners buying beds, crates, and dishes better suited to a Great Dane.

## BED

A dog bed can be as simple as a throw rug or as elaborate as a custom leather couch. Some Labs ignore beds; others love theirs. Yours is more likely to use one if he's not allowed on the furniture. Train him to go to his bed when you have company or don't want him underfoot. If you're going to be away, take the bed along to your boarding kennel so that your Lab has something that smells like home.

Weatherproof outdoor beds include those made out of the same material as patio cushions and are easy to clean with a hose. For hot weather, a raised bed made of pipe and plastic shade cloth allows airflow and will keep your canine

Dog beds come in a variety of colors and styles.

cool. Cooler pads, which are filled with cold water or cooled in the refrigerator, can be used indoors, outdoors, or in his crate. Plush pillow beds covered in washable fashion fabrics are filled with polyester fiberfill, foam rubber, or cedar chips. Cedar chips help repel fleas and combat odor. Wicker basket beds are fine for nonchewers but are way too tempting for a Lab who likes to gnaw while he relaxes. For senior dogs, heated or orthopedic beds filled with egg-crate foam provide comfort for aching joints.

Beds come in a variety of styles: bolster edges, flat slabs, beanbag, or donut style. Labs like to be cozy, and I find that they enjoy a bed that's not too big.

## COLLARS

A collar with a flat buckle or snap closure is the foundation piece of the Labrador wardrobe. Nylon collars come in every color and pattern imaginable. Leather collars are softer, and both types are available with fashion touches. I'm a big fan of bright fun collars for black Labs. So many people are afraid of big black dogs, and a cute collar makes them look like the friendly dogs they are. Think pink for a female black Lab—people will instantly smile when they meet her.

A head halter, which wraps over the nose and fastens behind the ears, is a type of walking collar that helps you control your Lab. It works just like a horse halter: You lead, your dog follows. Once he is used to it, you don't need much strength to control him. To introduce the head halter, attach two leashes, one to his flat collar and one to the halter. Be patient; he will try to paw it off at first, but after a few practice sessions he'll accept it.

Several types of no-pull harnesses are on the market now. In one style, the leash attaches to a hook on the front of the dog's chest. In another, movable bands loop up under his legs and fasten to the leash behind the shoulders. You'll notice that a Lab is often pictured on the front of the package!

## CRATE

Every Lab needs his own crate. He'll consider it his den and will often go in there on his own. Choose one that is just large enough for him to stand up and turn around in. He will feel cozy and safe in a crate that isn't too big. If you are just beginning to crate train, get a heavy-duty one. Thin wire, flimsy plastic, or fabric won't hold up to the power of a determined Labrador escape artist.

Beds or lightweight pads made to fit various sizes and brands of crates will help keep your canine comfy, but a young dog might chew them. Supervise your pup until you know he's not going to destroy his crate pad. Some puppies like having something to snuggle with; it's teenage dogs who are more likely to destroy their beds—and everything else, for that matter.

### MESH CRATES

Mesh crates are lightweight, fold flat, and are easy to carry. They are made of shade cloth and plastic or metal pipe. Air circulates through the mesh while providing shade, so they are perfect for family outings or dog shows. Once your dog is reliable in a crate and won't tear it up, I highly recommend fabric crates.

A collar with a flat buckle or snap closure is the foundation piece of the Labrador wardrobe.

### PLASTIC CRATES

If you plan to fly with your Lab, sturdy plastic crates are required. Most are labeled "airline approved," but check with the carrier to be sure before you decide on a particular brand.

### WIRE CRATES

Wire crates are portable and fold up for storage and transport. Air circulates through the wire and keeps your dog cool. Cover the crate with a blanket if you want to keep him warm or restrict his view (a great way to quiet him down if he is barking). Beautiful furniture-quality wood crate covers are available that match your decor and serve as end tables.

## DOG RUN

If you don't have a fenced yard, a kennel or dog run will keep Labby home and safe from predators. Most runs are made of chain link. It should provide shade and have a roof so that he can't jump or climb out. (Oh yes, they do . . .) The dog needs enough room to relieve himself without having to lie in his waste. He'll also need a water bowl or bucket that he can't dump and that won't freeze.

In climates with extreme weather, many people set up a dog run in their garage or basement so that their dog is indoors but not as confined as when he is in a crate.

## FOOD AND WATER BOWLS

I prefer a chew-proof stainless steel bowl with a rubber bottom that keeps it from skidding across the floor. Labs love to pick up their bowls and carry them around, and they quickly demolish plastic dog dishes. Once there are chew marks around the edge, it is hard to clean and sterilize plastic. Heavy ceramic bowls work well but are breakable. Many Labs play in their water bowls, so when my dogs are outside, I use a bucket that fastens to the fence with a clip. Metal buckets also resist chewing.

Veterinarians now recommend that you not feed large dogs from an elevated bowl. It used to be accepted that putting the dish on a platform would help prevent bloat, an emergency condition in which the stomach fills with gas and twists. Now experts recognize that dishes on raised platforms sometimes cause dogs to gulp more air, therefore increasing the risk of bloat rather than helping prevent it. For more information on bloat, see Chapter 6: Health of Your Labrador Retriever.

Labs love to pick up their food and water bowls and carry them around.

There are also bowls that will solve different problems. Ant-proof bowls have a reservoir around the outside that you fill with soapy water to repel bugs. Bowls to slow down speed-eaters have lumps in the bottom so that the dog has to eat around them.

## GATE

A pet gate limits your Lab's access to certain portions of the house, and it is a necessity during housetraining. If he learns to honor the gate when he is young, he won't be as likely to plow through it or jump over it when he's older.

The least expensive gates are expandable barriers that pressure-mount against the doorway with no screws or other permanent mounting hardware. To walk through them, you have to completely remove the gate, which is cumbersome. They are usually available in 24- or 30-inch (61- or 76.2-cm) heights, although I recommend the taller one.

If you are going to keep the gate up permanently, consider a more attractive wood or metal barrier. These mount permanently to the door frame and have a finger-trigger latch that easily opens with one hand. They come in colors and wood grain patterns to match your decor. Wider, freestanding barriers are available for large passages between rooms.

## GROOMING SUPPLIES

Your wash-and-wear Labrador needs some basic grooming supplies. For coat care, you'll need a slicker brush for regular use. During shedding season, you'll need a shedding blade, undercoat rake, and possibly a rubber curry. (See Chapter 5: Grooming Your Labrador Retriever for information on how to use these tools.)

Additional grooming supplies include toenail clippers, ear cleaner, flea comb, doggy toothbrush and toothpaste, and shampoo.

## IDENTIFICATION

A few pieces of identification will help your Lab find his way home should he ever become lost.

### ID TAGS AND LICENSE

Tags should include your name and telephone number, including the area code. Your mobile number is a better bet if you work or travel often. If the noise from rattling tags bothers you, order a collar with your phone number printed on it. Fabric tag holders also keep the tags from banging together.

Identification tags should include your name and telephone number, including the area code.

## MICROCHIP

If your dog escapes and is turned in to a shelter, he could be euthanized before you find him. A microchip is a permanent ID registered in a national database, which means that whoever finds him can find you before it's too late.

The microchip is implanted under the skin between the shoulder blades. It is tiny, no bigger than a grain of rice, and is imbedded in surgical glass to prevent infection.

**BE AWARE!**

In most counties, animal control will give a licensed dog a free ride home. At the pound, a purebred Lab is just another dog; he'll get no special treatment. If he gets picked up without a license, you will pay hefty fines. A license costs less for altered dogs.

When a lost dog reaches the shelter, a worker runs a scanner over him and the number appears, just like a UPC code on a product at the grocery store. When that number is entered into a computer, your contact information comes up.

Once your Lab is microchipped, you pay a once-in-a-lifetime fee (around $20) to a registry that keeps and updates your contact information for the life of the dog. Your veterinarian will give you the forms and registration information when she implants the chip. Most shelters and rescue groups implant a microchip when you adopt a dog.

Many brands of microchips are available. In recent years, universal ISO-compliant (International Organization for Standardization) scanners have been developed that read all brands and frequencies. Recently, in Southern California, a stray German Shepherd Dog was found to have a microchip registered in Italy. The owner was a serviceman who had brought the dog back to the United States. Because the dog was chipped, the owner was reunited with his dog.

Chips sometimes migrate down the dog's shoulder or leg, so have your dog scanned by the vet during his annual checkup to ensure that the chip is still in place.

## LEASH

For training and most uses I recommend a 4-foot (1-m) leather or cotton leash. While your Lab is still learning his leash manners, a short leash works best because it's easier to control him when he's closer to you. A 6-foot (2-m) leash is fine once your dog walks nicely without pulling. So if you start with a long leash, gather up the excess. Although chewable, leather and cotton are much easier on your hands than flat nylon, which will burn your hands if Labby pulls.

Like any other supplies for your Lab, the perfect leash would be chew-proof, but the only indestructible leash is a metal chain, which is hard to hang on to comfortably. I have found only one use for metal leashes: I use them as a tie-down in the house if a rowdy Lab is having trouble sitting still. I loop the handle around the couch leg, and the dog can't chew up the leash while he is tethered next to me.

If your Lab is well behaved and won't take off running when he spies a squirrel, retractable leashes allow him some leeway on walks to explore and sniff. If your Lab pulls, though, the case is awkward to hold, and he can easily yank it out of your hands. You'll end up on your face in the mud, and he'll be long gone. Use retractable leashes with care.

## TOYS

Labradors don't need fancy toys—they just need heavy-duty ones because they have vise-grip jaws. Some toys are safe for a short playtime, and then you should pick them up and put them safely away. Toys seem new and exciting if you rotate them, putting some away and then reintroducing them after about a week or so.

A leather or cotton leash (pictured here) is much easier on your hands than flat nylon.

My favorite Labrador toy is the Galileo bone, which is made of heavy rubber that lasts for months in spite of the most determined chewer. Many of the other rubber bones on the market break up in a matter of minutes. If you decide to give your Lab rawhides, hooves, or marrowbones, supervise him so that he doesn't swallow pieces too big to digest.

Stuffed with cheese, biscuits, liver sausage, or peanut butter, stuffable rubber toys will occupy your Lab when he has to be in his crate or left alone.

Freeze a stuffed toy to make the treats last longer. When used as a retrieving toy, they bounce in unexpected directions, unlike a ball. Floating models make great pool toys.

Heavy ropes made with fine string and knotted at the ends are fun for tug-of-war, retrieving, and chewing. Small bits of string will pass through your dog's system. Throw it away when the rope starts to come apart because big chunks can block his digestive tract.

Interactive or food-dispensing toys will entertain your Lab while feeding him. Fill them with his meal or treats, and he'll push the toy around to release the kibble. In multiple-dog homes, these might cause a fight, so they are best for an only dog.

Even if you don't hunt with your Lab, take advantage of his retrieving instinct by providing lots of fetch toys. Hunting catalogs offer canvas or rubber "bumpers." With a string tied at the end, you can throw them far enough to give your Lab a workout, and they float for water retrieves. Bumpers are usually white or bright orange so that you can find them if the dog doesn't.

Besides bumpers, Labs will fetch balls, sticks, stuffed animals, and just about anything that fits in their mouths. Empty plastic water jugs are fun, noisy, and cheap. My own Lab brought me an 8-foot (2-m) 2 x 4 (5 x 10 cm) and dropped it at my feet one day, hoping I'd throw it.

Labs love any kind of squeaky toy.

My Lab Tank's all-time favorite toy was a stuffed hedgehog squeaky toy; he carried it everywhere. I used it as a distraction when teaching him to retrieve an obedience dumbbell and tossed the hedgehog as a reward when he performed well. He loved it more than treats. When we moved to California from Seattle, every person in our obedience class gave Tank the same going-away gift: a stuffed hedgehog. We left town with a lifetime supply!

Tennis balls are a canine favorite but can be dangerous, blocking your dog's airway if he swallows one, so supervise and put them away between games. Hit the ball with a tennis racquet or other type of bat to send it farther than you can throw. We used to hit the ball over the house so that our dog could run around back and down the bank to the creek to fetch it. Labs also love to chew tennis balls to shreds, and many a dog has been left with his front teeth worn down to the gum line after years of gnawing.

I saved the best toy for last. Stuffed animals and anything with a squeaky in it are probably a Lab's favorite. They'll carry them around for a lifetime, even when there is no stuffing left. You'll quickly learn if these are too fragile for your Lab; it gets expensive to buy a new stuffed animal every week! And although garage sale stuffed toys are cheap, be sure to remove button eyes and other doodads that might be chewed off and swallowed.

## X-PEN

A folding portable wire fence, an x-pen (short for "exercise pen") works like a playpen. Adult Labs can easily knock it over or jump out, but if you introduce your dog to it when he is young, he'll learn to stay put. An x-pen is great for family picnics, dog shows, or other events where you don't want him running loose. Less confining than a crate, in an x-pen your Lab will feel like he's still part of the action.

Some of your dog's supplies will last a lifetime; some will last an hour. Keep in mind that the Labrador is a power chewer, and plan your shopping with that in mind.

# FEEDING YOUR
# LABRADOR RETRIEVER

**W**hile we enjoy variety in our food, with an ever-changing array of colors, textures, and flavors, our Labs happily devour the same thing day after day: kibble made with an endless list of mysterious ingredients. So how do we evaluate all that confusing information and pick the best food for our dogs?

My philosophy has always been: If it works, don't fix it. In other words, if your dog is healthy and a good weight, then there is no need to change his food. When in doubt, research different brands and their manufacturers until you find a company that you trust.

## NUTRITIONAL REQUIREMENTS FOR A BALANCED DIET

A healthy, balanced diet for your Lab contains these major nutrients: carbohydrates, fats, fiber, protein, vitamins and minerals, and water. The American Association of Feed Control Officials (AAFCO) establishes standards for the minimum and maximum levels of certain nutrients. Although all pet food manufacturers must provide the required nutrients, some use less expensive or lower-quality ingredients and manufacturing methods to meet the guidelines.

### CARBOHYDRATES

Carbohydrates are the sugars and starches that provide our Labs with their endless energy. The glucose provided by carbs also keeps their central nervous

In the appropriate amounts, fat is a vital nutrient, providing energy and contributing to healthy skin and hair.

systems healthy and functioning. Most dog foods are made with grain-based carbohydrates such as wheat, corn, oats, or white rice.

There is some evidence that food that is too high in cereal-grain carbohydrates can make your Lab hyperactive and incapable of sitting still or paying attention. If you have an abnormally active Lab, look into a food that has different carbohydrate sources and more animal protein as a possible alternative. Other grain-free sources of carbohydrates are potatoes, sweet potatoes, and yams.

## FATS

In appropriate amounts, fat is a vital nutrient, providing energy, contributing to healthy skin and hair, and moving nutrients and vitamins through the body. Essential fatty acids (EFAs) like omega-3 and omega-6 are often added to dog foods to help support the immune system and promote healthy cell function and circulation. If you are feeding a high-quality food to your Lab, there is no need to supplement his food with additional EFAs.

Labs who participate in strenuous work like hunting, agility, search and rescue, or flyball need to consume more fat. Alternatively, couch potato Labs easily get by on as little as 10 percent total fat in their diets. Most commercial foods, even those specifically formulated for Labs, contain fat in the 10 to 15 percent range.

Animal fats and vegetable oils are the fats most commonly used in dog food. Sprayed onto the kibble at the end of the manufacturing process, they are easy to digest and make the food taste good—sometimes too good. So many Labs are overweight that insufficient fat isn't usually a problem. On the other hand, a dog who doesn't get enough fat in his diet may have dry, itchy skin, low energy, and heart, circulation, or blood clotting problems.

## FIBER

Carbohydrates provide fiber, which helps your dog digest his meals and pass waste efficiently. Senior dogs in particular need more fiber in their diets to aid digestion. Fruits, potatoes, beans, and oatmeal are fiber sources that are easily fermented by bacteria in the large intestine. Cellulose, a component of plant cell walls, is another type of fiber but one that does not dissolve like other fiber sources. Because it absorbs water, it helps in stool formation and movement.

Proteins are the building blocks of the body and help provide energy.

Some manufacturers use low-quality fillers like peanut hulls, corncobs, and feathers to provide bulk and fiber. These are less expensive but are also less digestible and may aggravate the intestinal tract, causing discomfort and gas. If your Lab has excessive flatulence, figure out what fiber sources are in his food and avoid them in the future.

In recent years, contaminated fillers have resulted in pet food recalls involving major pet food companies.

## PROTEINS

Proteins are the building blocks of the body and are essential for healthy muscles, bones, skin, and hair. They also provide energy and help fight infections. The best protein sources for your Lab are meat and poultry.

Meat is listed in several forms on a dog food label, and each has a very different meaning. For example, meat or poultry "meal" usually names the specific source, such as beef, chicken, or lamb, unless several sources are used. Meal has the water removed and therefore provides more nutrients per pound (.45 kg) than fresh meat. The AAFCO defines chicken "meal" as a dry rendered meat that doesn't have other by-products. Meat "by-products" are defined by the AAFCO as those nonrendered parts of mammals that do not include meat; examples are blood, bone, and various organs. (Besides meat, manufacturers often use plant proteins—such as corn gluten meal or whole brown rice—because they are less expensive. Dogs, especially senior dogs, have difficulty digesting plant proteins, and Labs with grain allergies also react poorly to these ingredients.)

Dogs who suffer from protein deficiency may have dry skin and hair, with extreme shedding; ear infections; and a weak immune system.

## VITAMINS AND MINERALS

Although present in very small amounts, vitamins and minerals are essential to good health.

Vitamins contribute to the overall functioning of the body by providing antioxidants, assisting in the production of cartilage, improving eyesight, and other benefits. Vitamins are divided into two types: fat-soluble and water-soluble. The fat-soluble vitamins, A, D, E, and K, are stored in the liver and are toxic if a dog gets too much. Excess water-soluble vitamins (assorted B vitamins and vitamin C [ascorbic acid]) are eliminated in the urine, and while still risky, excess amounts do not pose as much danger.

Probably the most familiar mineral is calcium, which is critical for healthy bones. Calcium and phosphorus affect hormone levels and body functions like muscle contraction and nerve transmission. Other minerals affect a variety of internal canine processes, including thyroid function (iodine), production of red blood cells (copper), formation of hemoglobin (iron), maintenance of glucose levels and developing bones (manganese), carbohydrate metabolization (magnesium), support of immune and reproductive systems (selenium), and digestion (zinc).

## WATER

You may not think of water as a nutrient, but without it our dogs could not survive. Where other nutrient deficiencies show up over time, lack of water can have an immediate and fatal result. Be sure that your Labrador gets cool, fresh

# Dog Tale

The scent of a freshly grilled steak on a hot summer evening lured visiting Lab Chocolatté toward the patio table. He would never think of begging, but he positioned himself about 4 feet (1 m) away, at an equal distance between my husband and me. He then executed a perfect obedience school *sit*—alert, bright eyed, ears up and eager, and posed like a statue while he watched each bite travel from plate to mouth. The only thing that marred his performance and belied his impeccable manners was the blob of drool that made its way out of the corner of his mouth and slowly stretched all the way to the ground and settled in a puddle at his feet.

water every day. A moldy dish filled with week-old dirty water doesn't encourage him to drink, and dehydration causes a host of problems, from constipation to organ failure.

## HOW TO READ A DOG FOOD LABEL

The label is a marketing tool—the big type and pretty pictures are designed to sell you, the owner, on the food. If you really want to find out what is in your dog's food, read the fine print. The US Department of Agriculture (USDA) requires manufacturers to include certain information about the ingredients and nutrients on their packaging.

### TERMINOLOGY

The USDA and US Food and Drug Administration (FDA) specifically define the terminology you see, including the name of the food. A food cannot be labeled "organic" unless it meets stringent standards, for example. "Dinner" (or similar terms like "recipe," "formula," and "entrée") means that 25 percent of the weight (excluding water) must be the named ingredient. For instance, "Beef Dinner" must include 25 percent beef. "Dinner With Beef"—a slight change in wording—is only required to have 3 percent beef in the recipe. "Beef Flavored" food is not required to include any beef, but it must taste like beef.

### COMPLETE AND BALANCED

The label should include the statement "complete and balanced," which means that it is nutritionally adequate per AAFCO standards. The AAFCO also requires that the food be identified for "growth and lactation," "adult maintenance," or "all life stages." (There is currently no specification for senior food.) The label specifies that the food was tested with actual feeding trials or manufactured to meet AAFCO standards. In other words, not all foods are subjected to feeding trials, which are the generally preferred means of testing.

### GUARANTEED ANALYSIS

A "guaranteed analysis" statement, which lists minimum percentages of crude protein and fat and maximum percentages of fiber and moisture in that particular food, is also required. Other nutrients and additives may be listed, but this isn't required. The percentages themselves are not as meaningful as what makes up each of the nutrients. To get that information, you need to read the ingredients list.

## ORDER OF INGREDIENTS

Ingredients are listed in order from the most to the least by weight. There are some tricks to interpreting what you read. Although the first item might be meat, three out of the top five may be some sort of grain, so in reality there is probably more grain overall than meat in the food. Also, because meat contains a lot of water, it is naturally heavier. Once the water is removed, meat may not be the main ingredient after all. For example, it takes 5 pounds (2.3 kg) of chicken to make 1 pound (.45 kg) of chicken meal. So if "chicken meal" is the first ingredient, you are getting a larger proportion of actual chicken than if the first ingredient is "chicken."

## PRESERVATIVES

Chemical or natural preservatives are added to extend the shelf life of the food and must be listed on the label. Look for natural preservatives like citric acid and tocopherols (vitamin E). Less desirable are synthetic preservatives like BHT, BHA, and ethoxyquin.

## COMMERCIAL FOODS

The majority of pet owners feed commercially made dog food. There is a huge variety for you to choose from, and not all dog foods are created equal. Quality

If your senior Lab is not drinking enough water, canned food will help him get the moisture he needs.

varies depending on manufacturing methods and ingredient sources, which can even vary from batch to batch in the same brand. There is no perfect food. When making your choice, consider your dog's age, health, and activity level while striving to select a brand with the best nutrient sources.

### DRY FOOD

Most brands of dry food are extruded (cooked under pressure) and a few are baked, which is a more time consuming and expensive process. Heat destroys some beneficial nutrients, so fats and preservatives are usually sprayed on after cooking. Baked food is better for dogs prone to bloat because it won't swell up in the stomach after eating.

Dry food has a longer shelf life than canned or semi-moist foods. The price varies from inexpensive poor-quality foods to expensive premium brands but generally costs less per pound (.45 kg) than canned or semi-moist foods. Don't base your decision on price alone; the more expensive food may not be the best choice for your particular dog.

**BE AWARE!**

Treats are not meant to serve as a complete diet, and many contain additives that add flavor but also cause allergic reactions. Don't undo the positive results of all your careful research by feeding your Lab a bunch of junk food. Treats that look like steak or jerky may actually be mostly corn and sugar.

## CANNED FOOD

More expensive and not absolutely necessary, canned food still has its place in your Lab's menu. If your senior Lab is not drinking enough water, canned food will help him get the moisture he needs. Old dogs sometimes have trouble chewing, so adding wet food helps ensure that they are getting enough nutrition. Read the label because some canned foods are intended as a supplement rather than as a complete diet.

Sometimes dogs who eat wet food have bad breath. Canned food is also messier than dry food, and you should wash your Lab's bowl after every meal to prevent spoilage and avoid attracting bugs.

## SEMI-MOIST FOOD

Food manufactured to look like hamburger or sausage rolls makes owners happy but is so full of additives, artificial coloring, and sugar that it is not recommended for your dog. Reserve semi-moist food to use as an occasional treat, if at all.

## NONCOMMERCIAL FOODS

If your Lab has health problems (for example, allergies) that haven't been improved by traditional medicine, or if you just want him to eat healthier foods, consider a raw or home-cooked diet. Over the past 20 years, many owners have switched or are supplementing their dogs' food because they want control over the safety and quality of what they are feeding.

Raw or home-cooked foods need to provide the essential nutrients in the right proportions or you will cause more harm than good. Before you jump in, consult with a veterinary nutritionist to develop a proper balance of ingredients and supplements. Do your research, get balanced viewpoints, and don't believe everything you read on the Internet. Some people have a lot to say but no credentials.

Advantages of a raw or home-cooked diet:

- You don't have to feed 100 percent of one diet or another. Consider substituting one meal a day with premium commercial food so that your Lab gets sufficient vitamins and minerals.
- These diets don't usually contain chemicals, preservatives, or fillers, so dogs with allergies and food sensitivities tend to improve.
- You have control over the ingredients, their quality, and freshness.
- You can take advantage of seasonal vegetables.
- You can experiment until you have a combination that works for your dog.

Disadvantages of a raw or home-cooked diet:

- The ingredients are more expensive than commercial dog food.
- There is a high risk of contamination when handling raw meat.
- Research, shopping, and preparation are time consuming.
- Proper supplementation and achieving a nutritionally balanced diet is challenging.

Here's how to tell if a raw or home-cooked diet is good for your dog. After he has been fed the new diet for a few months, look for these signs:

- Examine the stool quality. Did he absorb the ingredients (good), or did they pass through his system without being digested (not good)?
- Is his coat glossy, dense, and richly colored? This is especially obvious in black Labs, who get faded, dry, or reddish-looking coats if they don't get proper nutrition.
- Are your Lab's eyes bright and shiny rather than dull or runny?
- Are his ears clean, or do they smell and look dirty or irritated?
- Are his teeth clean and his gums healthy?
- Does he have an appropriate amount of energy?

## RAW DIET

The BARF (Bones and Raw Food) movement started a trend toward feeding dogs the way wolves eat in the wild. Because wolves and wild dogs eat the entire animal—bones, feet, feathers, teeth, claws, and entrails—the theory is that this is how we should feed our pet dogs today.

One advantage to this diet is that the vitamins and minerals in raw ingredients won't be depleted by cooking. Also, raw bones exercise the dog's teeth and gums and provide calcium. (Cooked bones should never be fed to dogs, as they harden and splinter more easily than do raw and could perforate the intestine.) Monitor your dog's bowel movements when you change to raw. If you see splinters of undigested raw bones in the stool, then you should grind up the bones rather than feed them whole. Senior dogs may not digest raw food well because it is too high in fat and calories, which causes diarrhea and vomiting.

There are some risks to a raw diet. Take special care with raw meats because of the risk of *E. coli* or *salmonella* contamination, especially if there are children or immune-compromised adults in the house. If you are uncomfortable handling raw

Measure out your Lab's portion and feed him twice a day, on a schedule.

meat, buy frozen or dehydrated raw food at a specialty pet supply store or join a raw food co-op. Manufacturers of raw diets usually add fresh vegetables to the formula to provide a complete meal.

## HOME-COOKED DIET

Most home-cooked meals are a stew of meat, vegetables, greens, grain, and a small amount of oil. Remove the bones or grind them after cooking. Supplement this mixture with high-quality kibble or add your own mix of vitamins and minerals.

Home cooked does not mean table scraps! Most scraps contain too much fat, which can cause diarrhea, vomiting, and pancreatitis.

## HOW TO FEED: FREE-FEEDING VERSUS SCHEDULED FEEDING

Labs are notorious for overeating, so they are not usually candidates for free-feeding, a practice in which you leave a bowl of food down all the time. Measure out your dog's portion and feed him twice a day, on a schedule. Don't refill the bowl just because it is empty; wait until the next mealtime.

Two meals a day makes more sense for a Labrador, and there are advantages to regularly scheduled meals:
• Dogs are natural scavengers. Two meals a day prevent extreme hunger that

might cause your Lab to raid the trash, eat feces, chew, and indulge in other stress-related behaviors.

- Regular meals help with housetraining because it puts his digestive system on a schedule, especially if you leave him indoors while you are at work.
- You can regulate and monitor the amount of food he is eating.
- You can tell if your Lab isn't feeling well because you'll notice right away if his appetite is off.
- Two or even three meals a day help prevent bloat, an emergency situation in which the stomach twists and causes extreme pain and even death. (See Chapter 6.)
- Scheduled feeding reinforces your leadership role because you are the food provider.

### HOW TO SLOW DOWN A SPEED EATER

If your Lab is the Mario Andretti of eating, here are some tips to slow him down:
- Put large rocks (big enough that he can't swallow them) in his bowl so that he has to pick out his food. Some stores also sell bowls with raised bumps in the bottom. Or serve his food in a muffin tin. A spoonful in each cup will slow him down.
- Put his kibble in a food-dispensing toy. He'll still eat his full meal, but it will take more time to finish.
- Soak his food with water for a half hour before feeding. Wet food expands before it gets to the stomach, so he'll feel full sooner.
- Don't use a bowl. Just toss his ration on the floor and have him search for each bite. I know it sounds silly, but it works!
- Use a smaller bowl. So many people think of Labs as big dogs, so they buy a 5-quart (4.7-l) dish. Use that big dish for fresh water, and buy a bowl that holds about 2 cups of food.

### HOW MUCH TO FEED YOUR LABRADOR

When deciding how much to feed, take into consideration your dog's age, the

**BE AWARE!**
Specially formulated foods made exclusively for Labrador Retrievers are more marketing hype than science. Every dog's needs are different, even within the breed, so there is no one right food for every Lab. Some brands are extremely high in protein and fat content, which may be too much for the average Labrador who isn't working hard every day.

amount of exercise he gets, his general health, and the type of food you are feeding. The American Animal Hospital Association (AAHA) guidelines state that the amount could vary by as much as 30 percent higher or lower than label recommendations. So although reading the label is a good place to start, feed more if your dog is young and active. Your Lab needs less, as little as 1½ to 2 cups per day, if he is a couch potato. Don't forget to add treats and table scraps to his overall daily calorie count.

If you are buying a premium brand made with higher-quality ingredients, feed smaller meals. Better food is more digestible and your dog's body uses more of it, so he'll produce smaller stools.

When deciding how much to feed your Lab, take into consideration your dog's age, the amount of exercise he gets, his general health, and the type of food you are feeding.

## OBESITY

The Labrador Retriever was developed to work hard, and he has an appetite that matches his intended energy output. The original Labradors needed a layer of fat to protect them from the icy waters of the north Atlantic, and today's hunting dog also benefits from this fatty layer. But because most of us don't hunt or do other heavy physical work with our dogs, they don't need that extra weight. They need only enough food to match their activity level. And when your Lab is older, his appetite won't necessarily decrease, but he'll need fewer calories to keep him at a healthy weight. Labs are especially prone to hip dysplasia, and extra weight stresses joints and aggravates arthritis. Obesity is also hard on the heart and other organs.

## CHECK YOUR LAB'S WEIGHT

To check your Lab's weight, feel his rib cage. If you can't find his ribs, then he's too heavy. Look at him from the side; his tummy should tuck up a little behind his rib cage. From the top, does he have a waistline, or does his body shape go straight back or even bulge out? If he has no waistline, it's time for a diet.

## VISIT THE VET

Start with a visit to your veterinarian. The vet may run a series of blood tests to check for low thyroid levels, which often causes weight gain. Once that is ruled out, the doctor may suggest that you switch to a low-calorie, high-fiber food or even a prescription diet.

## CUT DOWN ON FOOD GRADUALLY

If you just go cold turkey and reduce your Lab's ration dramatically, his metabolism will decrease to compensate. Cut back gradually, over a period of days. If your Lab turns on the big sad eyes in an attempt to beg for more, add canned pumpkin, green beans, or other vegetables to make him feel full.

## FEED HEALTHIER FOODS

Healthy meals do no good if your dog is scarfing down junk food all day long. Labs are great beggars, and of course, fatty treats and table scraps also contribute to obesity. Treats should make up no more than 5 percent of his calorie intake. Switch to carrots, cooked sweet potatoes, or green beans as between-meal treats. If you use kibble for training or treats, subtract that amount from his meals.

## INCREASE EXERCISE

Just like people, diet and exercise help an obese dog lose weight. If your Lab is not exercising every day, it's time to go for walks and play fetch. Start slowly if he's uncomfortable or gets tired easily, and work up to several of sessions of activity every day.

Treats should make up no more than 5 percent of your dog's calorie intake.

# CHAPTER 5

# GROOMING YOUR
# LABRADOR RETRIEVER

L abrador Retrievers are a low-maintenance breed, but they do need regular brushing or you'll suffocate under mountains of dog hair during shedding season. The ears, eyes, toenails, and teeth also require attention, and caring for them should be part of your weekly routine.

## WHY GROOMING IS IMPORTANT

Grooming time is an opportunity for you to check your Lab from head to toe for health issues. As you brush, check for fleas, ticks, tumors, warts, infections, cuts, and abrasions. Look inside his ears to be sure that they are pink and healthy. Check for long, broken, or infected toenails and dewclaws (the toenail that is partway up the front legs) that have grown too long. Look between his toes for foxtails and burs. Check his paw pads for cuts or other injuries. Examine his mouth for broken teeth, excess tartar, and inflamed gums.

While you're working on your Lab, you are also enjoying one-on-one time with him. Grooming should be fun, not a chore, for both of you. Use treats when you are teaching him to tolerate grooming. Start slowly and reward small victories, like when he lets you open his mouth or cut one toenail.

## GROOMING SUPPLIES

- **Bristle brush:** Use as a finishing tool to sweep off any leftover hair after you groom. It is also gentle on his legs and tummy.
- **Nail clippers:** Clippers are usually guillotine style, with a sharp blade that squeezes shut. An alternative is a Dremel or similar tool that grinds down the nails instead of cutting.
- **Rubber curry:** A curry fits in the palm of your hand and has flexible rubber nubs. It loosens the undercoat and brings it to the surface.
- **Shampoo:** Labs don't require fancy shampoos. If your dog has dry or flaky skin, a medicated shampoo will help, but you need to figure out the underlying cause of the skin problem. Wash him with dog shampoo; those made for people dry out the coat and strip it of its natural oils.
- **Shedding blade:** A serrated shedding blade has rubber handles on either end and removes a lot

Wash your Lab with dog shampoo—those made for people will dry out his coat.

# Dog Tale

Sunday night was always time to trim toenails at my house. While I watched television, I'd get down on the floor with all four dogs, the clippers, and a bag of wonderful treats (like cheese or hot dog bits). The dogs would line up one at a time in front of me and hold out a paw. Tank always made sure that he was first, since food was involved. Clip, treat, clip and treat, down the row I'd go. When I finished the front paws, they'd each roll over for a belly rub and I'd clip, treat, clip and treat again on the hind feet until all the tummies were rubbed, the toenails shortened, and all the treats were gone.

of hair quickly as you pull it across the dog's coat. You may have to buy one at a horse supply/tack store or online.

- **Toothbrush:** Choose a doggy toothbrush or fingertip brush, which is a bristle-covered rubber sleeve that goes over the end of your finger.
- **Toothpaste:** Meat-flavored dog toothpaste tastes good and makes it easier to teach your Lab to tolerate brushing. Toothpaste made for people makes dogs seriously ill if they swallow it.
- **Undercoat rake:** This tool gets down into the coat and removes large amounts of undercoat during heavy shedding. Fine-toothed combs also get the undercoat out, but they tend to break outer guard hairs.
- **Wire slicker brush:** This is the main tool you'll need for grooming your Labrador. Most of the year it is the only tool you'll use for brushing, and it's also handy for quick touch-ups to remove loose hair.

## COAT AND SKIN CARE

Labs have a double coat that insulates them against cold and wet weather. The guard hairs (outercoat) are harsh and have natural oils that repel dirt and water. The undercoat is much softer and thicker and keeps the dog warm. Labs shed lightly year round and heavily every spring. Although the hair has some oil, a Lab's coat should never feel greasy, and he shouldn't have a doggy odor. If you see dandruff or greasy skin, something is wrong and it is time for a trip to the veterinarian.

To keep the coat at its best, regular brushing is about all a Lab needs. If he gets dirty, a quick rinse with the garden hose or a good brushing should clean him up. Too many baths dry out those natural oils and cause skin irritation.

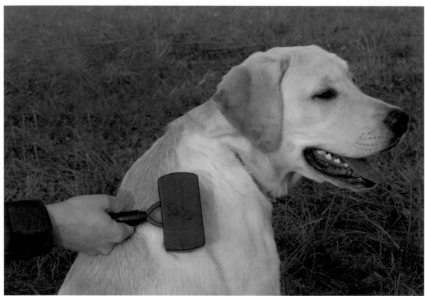

Brush your Lab outdoors if possible— it's much easier to clean up!

You should never shave your Lab. I know it is tempting when he's in full shedding mode, but his coat is his protection from heat, sun, and cold weather. Shaving won't prevent shedding; he'll still shed plenty as the new hairs grow in.

## BRUSHING

Regular brushing once or twice a week should keep minor shedding under control. When your Lab is "blowing coat" (losing a lot of hair), daily brushing will help minimize the mess. What you don't brush out will turn into fur bunnies in every corner, and the leftovers will weave into the fabric of your couch. You'll also wear dog hair to work every day.

Brush your dog outdoors—it's much easier to clean up.

### How to Brush

1. Use the rubber curry to loosen up his undercoat. Rub the curry deep into the coat in a circular motion and the fur will lift to the surface.
2. Go over his body with the slicker brush. Brush against the growth to take out even more hair. Be gentle in areas without much hair, like on the belly and legs.
3. Use the undercoat rake to loosen the stubborn, soft undercoat. There is a lot of thick hair over the shoulders, so part it with your hand to get down to the roots. You'll also remove a lot from his neck and under his ears.

4. Use the shedding blade and wire slicker brush to pick up loose hair.
5. Finish up with a bristle brush if you'd like. Use it on the legs and tummy to gently remove loose hair from tender parts of his body.

## BATHING

Your Lab should only need a bath once or twice a year unless he gets into something really stinky. On the rare occasion that Labby needs a bath, here's how to go about it.

### How to Bathe

Whether you bathe him out in the yard or in the bathtub, use lukewarm water because hot water dries out the coat.
1. Put cotton balls in his ears to keep water and shampoo out.
2. Soak your Lab thoroughly, getting him wet through the thick coat and down to the skin. (This could take a while.) Use a powerful nozzle or shower massager to penetrate the outercoat.
3. Soap and massage him with dog shampoo. Use the curry to work the shampoo in and get loose hair out.
4. Use a cloth on his face and ears. Take care not to get shampoo in his eyes.
5. Rinse thoroughly until the water runs clear. A Lab's water-repellant coat makes it difficult to get all the shampoo out, but if you leave any shampoo on him, it will irritate his skin.

6. Let him shake, then rub him down with towels to remove the excess water. Remove the cotton balls and be sure to dry his ears well.

Labs are drip-dry; they usually don't need to be blow-dried unless it's winter or you want to blow out excess hair. Blow dryers made for humans get very hot, so only use the low setting. Better still, use a dryer meant exclusively for dogs.

After any bath, a Lab's first instinct is to roll around on

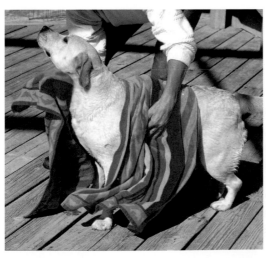

After your Lab's bath, rub him down with towels to remove the excess water.

the ground, so either confine him in his crate with some dry towels or let him roll on the lawn so that he'll stay halfway clean. If you're in the house, he'll want to rub his head and body along the walls and against the couch, so be prepared!

## DENTAL CARE

Just like people, dogs need to brush their teeth regularly to prevent plaque buildup and gum disease. Because they can't do it themselves, it is our job to do it for them. When you brush your Lab's teeth, you have the opportunity to check for bad breath, broken teeth, gum disease, and tumors.

Symptoms of gum disease (gingivitis) start as early as two years of age. Inflammation starts where the teeth meet the gums. As gingivitis progresses, pockets form in the gums, next to the teeth. Food and bacteria get stuck in these pockets and cause periodontal disease, the most common cause of tooth loss in dogs. If not treated, infections can spread throughout the body and cause disease and organ failure. That's why taking care of your Lab's teeth is so important.

Several types of doggy toothbrushes are available. Besides a regular canine toothbrush, which has a short handle, try a fingertip toothbrush. Or just wrap your finger with some gauze.

### HOW TO CARE FOR THE TEETH

1. Most dogs will resist when you first try to brush their teeth, so go slowly and just rub your Lab's gums at first with a little doggy toothpaste and with your bare finger without trying to open his jaws. He'll learn to like the taste and sensation.
2. Roll back the edge of his lips and brush the teeth and gum line using small circles, holding the bristles at a 45-degree angle.
3. Next, gently open his mouth and brush the backs of his teeth using the same circular motion.

Inspect your dog's teeth for signs of infection and decay.

Regular dry food is not enough to keep a dog's teeth and gums in good condition, so look for teeth-cleaning treats and specially made toys to supplement your cleaning efforts. If your dog's mouth is healthy, brushing two to three times a week should be sufficient, although daily brushing is ideal. If your Lab is suffering from gingivitis, brush daily to massage his gums and encourage healing.

You'll still need to have a veterinarian clean your Labrador's teeth at some point, but your dog will suffer less pain and be under anesthesia for less time because his teeth have had regular care. The vet will scale and polish the teeth and clean below the gum line where normal brushing doesn't reach. She will also perform any needed extractions and conduct a thorough mouth exam.

## EAR CARE

Centuries ago, man started selectively breeding wolves for desirable characteristics, eventually creating the dog and its many breeds. While wild wolves had upright ears, some dog breeds developed floppy ears. One of the unintended consequences of drop ears is that they restrict air from entering the ear canal, creating a dark, damp environment—the perfect place for trouble to start.

After a swim, dry your Lab's ears because there isn't enough air circulation under the flaps to dry completely on their own. After he goes running in tall grass, weeds, or brush, check for foxtails and the seeds of other grasses that might eventually work their way down into the inner ear and cause infection. Also, look in his ears for ticks and remove them.

If the ears are inflamed or have a dark reddish brown or black substance in them, it could be an infection or ear mites. Smell the ears; a bad odor means there's a problem. Your Lab's ears need attention if he shakes his head, scratches his ears, holds his head at an odd angle, or won't let you touch his head.

Some Labs are prone to regular fungus or yeast infections in their ears. Allergies also cause redness and irritation, which may lead to an infection.

A well-groomed dog is a happy dog.

## HOW TO CLEAN THE EARS

For a dog with healthy ears, clean once a week at most. Too much cleaning is harmful; dogs need some wax to protect the inner ear. Also, avoid poking swabs down into the ear because you could push bacteria or foreign objects farther into the ear canal and damage the eardrum. If your Lab is suffering from an infection, your veterinarian will deep clean his ears and prescribe an ointment to apply until the problem clears up. If your dog has recurring ear problems, ask your vet for some ear wash, and clean more often.

To clean your Lab's ears:

1. Use a cotton ball or wrap your finger with some gauze. Add a few drops of mineral oil if the ears are especially dirty.
2. Wipe the inside of the ear, starting at the inside and wiping outward so that the dirt isn't pushed farther into the ear.
3. Finish up with a dry cotton ball or piece of gauze to remove any remaining moisture.

## EYE CARE

The Labrador Retriever's eyes need very little care.

### HOW TO CARE FOR THE EYES

1. Wipe out any gunk that gets stuck in the corners.

2. If his eyes are runny or red around the edges, check to see if there is a piece of grass stuck under the eyelid.
3. If the irritation persists, take him to the vet; if he has scratched the surface of his eye, he'll need prescription eye drops to ease the pain and help it heal.

If your Lab's eyes look cloudy or bluish, that could be a sign of cataracts. See Chapter 6 for information about eye diseases in Labradors.

## NAIL CARE

If you hear a tippity tap as your Lab trots across your hardwood floor, it's time to trim his toenails. When allowed to grow too long, nails throw a dog's legs and joints out of alignment, which affects how he stands and walks. Besides scratching your floors, long toenails will also snag the carpet and leave scratches on your arms when Labby plops a paw on you to ask for a game of fetch.

A dog who is outside running a lot, especially on hard surfaces, wears his nails down, but you should still check them weekly for excess growth. Dogs who don't get a lot of exercise don't wear down their nails and need more frequent trimming. Also, nail growth varies from dog to dog. For example, a senior dog's nails grow faster if he is taking glucosamine supplements.

You probably won't be able to just sit down and start clipping toenails. Most Labs will snatch their feet away and wiggle endlessly until they learn how to sit still for clipping. While you are teaching your dog to tolerate toenail clipping, you're also teaching him to allow you to handle his feet. An added bonus: In bad weather, you'll be glad he lets you dry off the wet mud, snow, and ice that collects between his toes.

### HOW TO TRIM THE NAILS

Use really sharp clippers, and change the blades often. Dull blades don't make a clean cut and they split or tear the nails.

1. Start with short sessions. Make nail trimming a game and reward your Lab for allowing you to mess with his feet.
2. Run your hand down his leg and foot and give him a treat before he yanks his foot away. Try to deliver the treat while your other

**BE AWARE!**

Don't forget to clip your Lab's dewclaws, the toenail that is partway up his front legs. Some breeders remove the dewclaws at birth, but many Labs still have them. If not trimmed, the dewclaw grows in a circle and imbeds itself in the leg, causing infection and severe pain.

hand is still touching his foot so that you're rewarding the touch, not the take away. Gradually lengthen the time you hold the foot.

3. Once he lets you touch all four feet without a problem, massage his legs and his feet between the toes.

4. Touch his toenails with the clippers and remove them quickly without cutting.

5. Finally, clip a tiny bit, not even 1/32 of an inch (.08 cm). Make a vertical cut, not angled. It may take a few days before your dog allows you to clip more than one or two toenails. Try a different foot each session. Follow each clip with a treat.

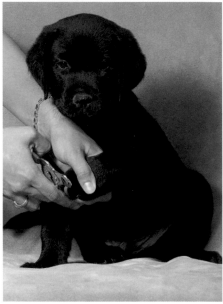

When trimming your Lab's nails, start with short sessions and make it a game that yields rewards.

If you cut the nails too short, you'll cut into the quick, which is a vein filled with blood that runs down the middle of the nail. In a yellow Lab, the pinkish quick is visible through the nail. On a black or chocolate Lab, you can't see the quick, so stay on the safe side and cut less.

If you cut the quick and the toenail starts to bleed, stick your finger against the end of the nail and apply pressure to stop the bleeding, which could take up to five minutes. Put styptic powder (available at pet supply stores) on the end of the nail to prevent further blood loss. Restrict your Lab's activity for an hour or more so that it doesn't start bleeding again. He'll be reluctant to get hurt again, so you may have to do some retraining.

If your dog hasn't had his nails clipped recently, the quick will extend nearly to the end of the nail. Trim tiny bits each day and work the nails back gradually, which will make the quick recede. Ultimately, the end of his toenail should be even with the end of his toe. It may take several weeks to get to this point.

An alternative to using clippers is a grinder. You sand down the end of the nail with an abrasive cylinder on the end of a handheld grinder. Acclimate your dog to the sound and feel of this tool, just like you did with the clippers. The grinder gets hot, so stop every few seconds and put finger pressure against the end of the nail to cool it and relieve the vibrating sensation.

## FINDING A PROFESSIONAL GROOMER

Why would you ever take a Lab to a groomer? Although they rarely need bathing, even Labs occasionally need professional help in the following situations:

- If you or someone in your household has allergies, have a groomer blow out excess undercoat during shedding season. A groomer's industrial-strength blow dryers are more powerful than those you have at home.
- If you aren't comfortable trimming your Lab's nails, have a groomer do this chore for you.
- If your Lab gets skunked, a groomer will use high-powered sprayers and special odor-eater shampoos that will clean him all the way to the skin.

Ask your dog-owning friends for referrals to a local groomer. When choosing a grooming shop, consider these issues:

- Beware of groomers who leave dogs in a crate with dryers blowing, where it quickly gets too hot to be safe. A handheld dryer is safer and more effective.
- Check to see that shop is clean. As the day goes on, there will always be hair and grooming debris around, but do staff members sweep up regularly?
- Do they disinfect or at least sweep off the table between dogs?
- Check that dogs are not left unattended on grooming tables. A dog left with his neck in a grooming noose could strangle if he jumps off the table.
- Is the shop escape-proof? Some groomers leave the front door open on hot days; could your dog run out the door, or is there a barrier?

- Do the groomers treat the dogs well? Do they try to make a dog comfortable with his surroundings?
- Where is your dog kept while he is waiting for you to pick him up?
- Do they provide water or walk the dogs if they are there for several hours?
- How do they deal with difficult dogs who don't want their toenails trimmed?

An alternative is to hire a mobile groomer who comes to your house and bathes your dog in a van out in the driveway. Then your Lab doesn't have to spend the day in an unfamiliar, noisy place.

Ask your dog-owning friends for referrals to a local groomer.

# CHAPTER 6

# HEALTH OF YOUR
# LABRADOR RETRIEVER

Labrador Retrievers are a generally healthy breed and live 12 to 14 years. Like any dog, they are subject to a variety of genetic conditions, injuries, and illnesses. However, your Lab will live a longer, healthier life if you follow a schedule of regular preventive care and take proactive steps to ensure his well-being.

## FINDING A VET

If you don't already have a veterinarian, ask your breeder and other Labrador owners who live near you for a referral. Friends, local trainers, and boarding kennel staff also know the inside story on local vets.

Your state's veterinary medical association should have an online listing of members in your area. National databases, such as the American Animal Hospital Association (AAHA) (www.healthypet.com), also list accredited practices.

One way to find a vet you can trust and communicate with is to schedule a visit and interview the veterinarians and the staff. Will they take time to answer your questions and explain things so that you understand? Will you be able to see the vet of your choice? What are the doctors' backgrounds and specialties? Are they experienced with Labradors? What kinds of health problems have they treated?

While you are there, check that the facility is clean and well maintained. Also consider whether the hours are convenient for you and what happens in an off-hours emergency.

Ask your breeder and other Labrador owners who live near you for a vet referral.

## THE ANNUAL VET VISIT

Once your Lab is past the puppy stage, he needs a yearly wellness exam. Dogs are experts at hiding pain, and you may not see symptoms of a major illness until it is too late. If your veterinarian discovers a disease in its early stages, something serious might be cured. Over the years, the vet develops a history of blood tests, weight, and other information about your Lab, and she'll be able to recognize and evaluate changes in your dog's condition.

The exam is also an opportunity for your veterinarian to:

- update vaccines
- conduct an annual heartworm test
- adjust or renew prescriptions
- examine the teeth and gums
- check a stool sample for parasites
- answer your questions about health and behavior

**BE AWARE!**

The bordetella vaccine is available in two forms: intranasal or injection. It protects against kennel cough and some—but not all—upper respiratory infections. Most kennels require that the vaccine be administered at least five days before you bring your dog in for boarding and require a booster every six months.

## VACCINATIONS

In the first weeks of a puppy's life, his mother's milk passes on antibodies to protect him from disease. Once weaned, it is time for his first vaccines because his mother's antibodies are no longer protecting him. You might think that vaccines for diseases like distemper aren't necessary or are old-fashioned because you haven't heard of any sick dogs in years. Visit any animal shelter and talk to the staff, and they will tell you that they often have outbreaks among the dogs in their care. Canine diseases aren't seen much in the general public because responsible owners have been diligent about vaccinating their dogs. Unprotected dogs are extremely vulnerable.

The core vaccines recommended for every dog are for distemper, hepatitis, parvovirus, and parainfluenza (DHPP), usually combined in a single injection. The initial DHPP vaccine, at six to eight weeks, primes the puppy's system to develop antibodies that protect his immune system from disease. Boosters are administered at 9 to 11 weeks, 12 to 14 weeks, 16 weeks, and then a year later. At the 16-week appointment, he'll receive his first rabies vaccine, which will also need a booster in a year.

After the first year, the AAHA recommends a booster for the core vaccines once every three years. Additional vaccines that you should discuss with your veterinarian are for Lyme disease (a disease transmitted by ticks), bordetella (also known as kennel cough), coronavirus (an intestinal infection), and leptospirosis (a bacterial disease).

## SPAYING AND NEUTERING

Female dogs are spayed, which means that the uterus and ovaries are removed. Shelter dogs are spayed as early as six weeks, but a pet can wait until between four and eight months of age, before her first heat cycle (when she is capable of being bred). Your vet will removes the stitches 10 to 14 days after the surgery.

Male dogs are neutered, meaning the testicles are removed. This is an external surgery unless one of the testicles hasn't descended from the abdominal cavity. Your Lab will be up and bouncing, ready to play the next day, but walk him on leash for a few days so that he doesn't open his incision. Males can be neutered at any time, but owners usually wait until four to six months of age.

If you bought a puppy who is not a potential show dog, chances are the breeder required him to be altered before you received the American Kennel Club (AKC) papers, and the registration certificate is a "limited registration." Your dog is still an AKC-registered Labrador and eligible to compete in performance events.

Every pet dog should be spayed or neutered. Only the best of the best Labrador Retrievers should be bred. There is no excuse for breeding dogs who might carry unknown genetic diseases or other faults, like poor temperament. Poorly bred Labs also contribute to a loss of "type" in the breed, meaning they start looking like other breeds and don't have distinctive Labrador characteristics anymore. Hundreds of thousands of Labs

Once your Lab is past the puppy stage, he needs a yearly wellness exam.

are born every year, so there is no shortage of dogs to meet public demand.

- Altered dogs get along better in a multi-dog household.
- Breeding and raising a litter is expensive. The stud fee, health screenings, vet visits, worming, registration, and other expenses add up quickly. If the bitch (female) has problems delivering, she may need a cesarean section surgery to save her and her puppies. She is also at risk for infections and complications during and after delivery.
- Unaltered female Labs are more susceptible to mammary or uterine cancer and pyometra (an often fatal uterine infection). Unneutered males are at risk for prostate and testicular cancer.
- Intact dogs are much more likely to roam and fight. Because males smell a female in heat up to 3 miles (4.8 km) away, your Labrador may dig out or climb fences in his frenzy to breed.
- Can you place all of the puppies in permanent homes? Labs have ten or more puppies in a litter, and a responsible breeder guarantees to take the puppies back at any time during their lives if the buyers can't keep them.
- All breeding dogs should be screened for inherited diseases like hip and elbow dysplasia and progressive retinal atrophy (PRA). This is expensive and time-consuming, and you should be prepared to forego breeding if your dog is affected or is a carrier. Labrador rescue groups across the United States take in thousands of purebred Labs every year, many with congenital health problems that could have been avoided by selective breeding.
- Are you a member of a Labrador breed club? Do you have a network of breeders and experts that will mentor you and help ensure that you are doing the best for the breed?
- Has your dog achieved a conformation championship or a hunting title? These accomplishments prove that he has physical characteristics that conform to the breed standard and that he is able to do the work Labs were developed to do.

## PARASITES

Fleas, ticks, mites, and worms probably make your skin crawl just thinking about them. Now think of the poor dog who has to suffer with them in and on his body. Some of these parasites can be transmitted to humans too, so you'll want to prevent them before they get a foothold on your Lab.

### FLEAS AND TICKS

Twenty years ago, life with dogs meant a constant battle against fleas and ticks.

Check your Lab for fleas and ticks after he's been playing outside.

Today they are easy to prevent. Fortunately, either spot-on or monthly oral preventives protect our canine buddies from both of these external parasites.

Fleas feed on your dog's blood and multiply quickly, taking over your house and yard. If you see tiny bugs crawling on your dog near the head, base of the tail, or on the belly, they are probably fleas. Small black and white specks on his skin are flea droppings and eggs. Dogs scratch themselves frantically to try to relieve the itching caused by fleabites. Fleas can also cause anemia and secondary skin infections that require antibiotic treatment.

Ticks transmit serious diseases like Rocky Mountain spotted fever and Lyme disease. Like fleas, they feed on your dog's blood. Any time your Lab is out hiking with you in fields or on trails, he could pick up ticks. A feeding tick embeds its head in the dog's skin and fills with blood. At this point he hangs off your dog's body and looks like a big grape. He may remain attached for several days.

After outdoor excursions, check Labby's body, head, and ears for ticks and remove them before they embed themselves in his skin. A loose tick is easy to pick off, but you must crush it or drop it in a jar of alcohol or he'll just hop back on. To remove an attached tick, use tweezers and grasp the tick at his head against the dog's skin. If you pull just the body, the head will break off and remain embedded. Pull it out without twisting. Clean the area and apply a triple antibiotic ointment or similar first-aid cream to soothe the skin irritation.

## GIARDIA, COCCIDIA

Because many Labs hunt, they are at risk for infection by these single-celled parasites, which are ingested through infected water or soil. The most obvious symptom is bloody or watery diarrhea. Wash your hands frequently to prevent transferring the parasites to you or other family pets. Bring clean drinking water with you if you take your dog hunting or camping.

## HEARTWORMS

Once confined primarily to the South, heartworm now affects dogs throughout the United States. When a mosquito bites an infected dog, it ingests blood containing heartworm microfilariae (larvae). When it bites the next dog, it injects the microfilariae into the dog's bloodstream, where they mature into heartworms and attack the pulmonary arteries. Your dog may show no symptoms at all, or he may have a dry cough, lose weight, and ultimately suffer from lung problems and congestive heart failure.

Heartworm is easy to prevent and difficult to treat. Your Lab should have an annual blood test and be on a daily or monthly preventive. Some preventives also kill other parasites, so your Lab gets some bonus protection. If a dog gets heartworm, the treatment is grueling. In addition to receiving severe arsenic-based medication, he'll be confined to complete crate rest for several weeks.

## BE AWARE!

Although the amount varies before an item causes a toxic reaction, the following foods are poisonous to dogs:
- alcoholic beverages
- avocado, peach, cherry, and apricot pits
- chocolate
- coffee and tea
- foods prepared with the artificial sweetener xylitol
- grapes and raisins
- onions and onion powder
- walnuts and macadamia nuts

## MITES

Three common health conditions—ear mites, demodectic mange, and sarcoptic mange—are caused by mites.

### Ear Mites

Ear mites often cause a bacterial or yeast infection in the ears and are also contagious to other dogs and cats in your household. A veterinarian can identify them under a microscope and prescribe medication to kill the mites. Allergies can also cause ear infections, so get an accurate diagnosis before you start treatment.

## Demodectic Mange

Demodectic mange (demodicosis) is transferred from a mother to her puppies and is not contagious to humans. Hair loss and red and scaly skin are symptoms. The disease usually resolves without treatment by the time the dog is a year old. For more severe cases, miticidal dips or ointments may be prescribed. Secondary infections are common.

## Sarcoptic Mange

Sarcoptic mange is also known as scabies and causes intense itching from the mites burrowing into the dog's skin. The mites are contagious to people and cats. Symptoms include itching and red bumps, often on the ears, back of the forelegs, and underside of the body. Isolate an infested dog and treat the condition with shampoos and miticidal dips. Some worming medications also kill the mites.

## ROUNDWORMS, WHIPWORMS, HOOKWORMS, TAPEWORMS

Deworming is a routine part of puppy care, but roundworms, whipworms, and hookworms infect adult dogs too. The only way to diagnose them is to have your vet examine a stool sample under a microscope. Evidence of tapeworms is easy to see with the naked eye—small segments that look like grains of rice stick to the fur near the dog's anus. Fleas, lice, and mice transfer tapeworms to dogs. Treatment varies depending on the type of worms present.

# DISEASES AND INJURIES IN LABRADOR RETRIEVERS

Dr. Fran Smith, DVM, chairperson of the health committee for the Labrador Retriever Club, Inc. (the AKC parent club in the United States), and president of the Orthopedic Foundation for Animals (OFA) states that Labs are one of the healthiest dog breeds. She comments that there are so many more Labs than any other breed that you hear more about hereditary ailments, even though most conditions rarely occur.

Although Labs are healthy overall, there are a few conditions you should be aware of so that you ensure that any puppy you purchase is not affected. If a breeder tells you she's "never seen it" in her dogs, that is not a guarantee of good health. If the sire and dam both carry the gene for a particular condition, they might produce puppies with the disease and therefore should never be bred at all. The breeder won't know that her dogs are carriers unless she tests the dogs prior to breeding.

## ALLERGIES

If you live in a warm climate, your Lab is more likely to suffer from allergies and skin problems. Dogs can be sensitive to pollen, mold, fleas, a food ingredient, or a multitude of other triggers. Symptoms include scratching, licking the feet, ear infections, and dry, flaky skin. All of this irritation sometimes leads to secondary skin infections that require treatment.

Symptoms of allergies include dry, flaky skin and scratching.

You can prevent flea infestations, but figuring out other allergy sources is more difficult. Your veterinarian may recommend that you visit a veterinary dermatologist for further testing. If a food allergy is identified, switch to a brand that doesn't include that ingredient. Sometimes all you can do is treat the symptoms to keep your Labrador comfortable. In extreme cases, desensitizing shots or daily medication can help prevent flare-ups.

## BLOAT/GASTRIC DILATATION VOLVULUS (GDV)

Most pet owners have heard of bloat because it affects many large breeds, but it is rarely seen in Labs. The dog's stomach fills with gas and then twists, which stops blood circulation and can quickly be fatal. Signs of bloat include a swollen abdomen, trying to vomit, and restlessness.

If you think that your Lab may be bloating, take him to the vet immediately. Fluid therapy and relieving the gas may keep the situation from getting worse. If the stomach has already twisted, surgery is necessary to save his life.

## CENTRONUCLEAR MYOPATHY (CNM)

Also called hereditary myopathy, this condition causes muscle weakness, and an affected dog cannot exercise normally. Symptoms include physical weakness, abnormal posture like a hunched back, a "bunny hop" gait, and exercise intolerance. The disease can be managed but there is no cure. A genetic test is available to screen for this disease.

## COLD WATER TAIL

After a cold swim or bath, your Lab's tail may hang straight down and limp rather than up and wagging. Called by various names such as "limber tail," this is a muscle sprain and is more common in hunting dogs because they are in the water and exercising heavily. It is painful and lasts for several days before the tail returns to its normal position. Anti-inflammatory drugs will ease your Lab's discomfort in the meantime.

After a cold swim, your Lab's tail may hang straight down and limp, a condition called cold water tail.

## CRUCIATE LIGAMENT INJURY

Labs are prone to tearing their anterior cruciate ligaments (ACL), which are located in the rear knee joints. Sudden twisting and turning, often while playing fetch, cause the rupture. Overweight dogs are especially susceptible, and dogs who have torn the ACL in one leg often end up tearing the ACL in the other as well. The tear must be repaired surgically, and recovery time is 6 to 12 weeks.

## ELBOW DYSPLASIA

Loose bone chips, arthritic changes, and loss of cartilage in one or both front elbow joints make an affected dog limp and show signs of pain, especially after exercise. Symptoms of elbow dysplasia can appear in dogs as young as four months old. Treatment includes weight control and moderate exercise like walking, which helps keep the joints flexible and improves the dog's strength. Some cases require surgery to remove the bone chips.

## EXERCISE-INDUCED COLLAPSE (EIC)

Exercise-induced collapse syndrome is often seen in young, high-energy Labrador Retrievers. The dog staggers, loses control of his rear legs, and collapses in the midst of what appears to be normal exercise. Most dogs are fine within 5 to 20 minutes. Some dogs have died during an incident of EIC, but an affected Lab can live a normal life as long as you limit exercise and stop immediately if he appears uncoordinated or wobbly on his feet. EIC carriers are identified by a genetic test. There is no cure for EIC. In most cases, limiting exercise and excitement are the only recommended ways to prevent another incident.

## HIP DYSPLASIA

This is a crippling and all-too-common disease in Labs. In susceptible dogs, the head of the femur fits poorly into the hip socket and causes pain, lameness, and arthritis. A dog with mild hip dysplasia can be kept more comfortable with pain-relieving drugs and nonweight-bearing exercise like swimming. Maintaining a lean to moderate weight also reduces stress on the joints. Some affected dogs live their entire lives with no symptoms at all. For more serious cases, complete hip replacement is necessary. Another surgical option is triple pelvic osteotomy (TPO), where the surgeon cuts the pelvic bone into three pieces and rotates the hip. Both are major operations and require a long recovery period, up to several months.

Both hip and elbow dysplasia are preventable. Both parents should be X-rayed, declared clear of the disease, and should have a clear pedigree for several generations before they are bred. The results should be registered with the OFA, which grades the hips and elbows from severely dysplastic to excellent.

## OSTEOCHONDRITIS DISSECANS (OCD)

Young, rapidly growing males between six and nine months of age are most likely to suffer from OCD. The cartilage in the shoulder joint breaks off and results in loose pieces that irritate the joints and cause pain. Although a genetic

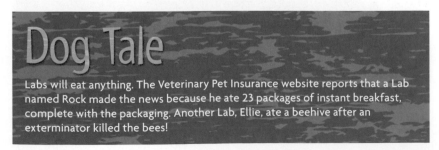

Dog Tale

Labs will eat anything. The Veterinary Pet Insurance website reports that a Lab named Rock made the news because he ate 23 packages of instant breakfast, complete with the packaging. Another Lab, Ellie, ate a beehive after an exterminator killed the bees!

component exists, experts suspect that two practices might aggravate or even cause OCD. First, running on hard surfaces or jumping causes trauma to joints and bones that aren't fully developed. Second, food formulated for rapid growth weakens bones. If the damage is minor, six weeks or more of crate rest will allow the bone to heal and form new cartilage. A faster solution is surgery to remove the bits of loose cartilage.

## PANOSTEITIS

Your teenage Lab (6 to 14 months) may suddenly appear lame and sore on one front leg and the next day on the other. This "wandering lameness," also called growing pains, is inflammation in the long bones of the front legs and appears in larger breeds like Labradors. Pano eventually goes away without treatment, but it is very painful, so anti-inflammatory drugs and crate rest are recommended until the condition disappears.

## PROGRESSIVE RETINAL ATROPHY (PRA)

The form of PRA in Labrador Retrievers is called progressive rod-cone degeneration (PRCD), meaning that the rod and cone cells of the retina develop normally but gradually degenerate and cause complete blindness. Symptoms usually start between four and seven years of age, and the first sign

Labs can suffer from a few inherited eye diseases, such as retinal dysplasia.

of the disease is often night blindness. There is a genetic test for PRA, and the Canine Eye Registry Foundation (CERF) maintains a database of eye exam results.

## RETINAL DYSPLASIA

More common in Labradors than PRA, this is also an inherited disease and the effects on the dog's vision depend on how severely he is affected. A type of retinal malformation where the layers of the retina do not form together properly, it can range from small blind spots that the dog doesn't even notice to a completely detached retina where the dog is totally blind. It is not a progressive disease, so an affected dog's condition will not deteriorate. A board-certified veterinary ophthalmologist should examine any dog who will be used for breeding, starting as young as 12 weeks of age and annually thereafter. Breeders should provide prospective puppy buyers with CERF results stating that both parents' eyes are normal.

## TRICUSPID VALVE DYSPLASIA (TVD)

TVD is the most common heart disease occurring in Labs. Present at birth, it is a defect in a valve on the right side of the heart. A heart murmur and signs of congestive heart failure are the first indications of the disease. Puppy buyers should have their vet check for a murmur during the first exam. There is no cure or treatment for TVD, but vets may prescribe diuretics to relieve excess fluid retention and recommend restricting exercise to avoid stressing the heart too much. Breeders should provide buyers with evidence of a clear heart exam from both parents.

# MEDICAL INSURANCE

Advanced treatments have been developed for many canine diseases, and those that previously caused a dog's death may now be treatable and curable. In addition, typical Lab mishaps like swallowed rocks and porcupine encounters will surely happen at least once in your dog's life. Some of these treatments are expensive, and today many owners purchase pet insurance to protect them from catastrophic expenses when their dog is ill or injured.

Companies offer a wide range of premiums, deductibles, and terms. Policy options range from major medical coverage with a large deductible to comprehensive plans that include preventive care and vaccines.

## ALTERNATIVE THERAPIES

When traditional Western medicine isn't working or when people want to use natural substances and methods to treat their dogs, they often try alternative therapies. As scientists have begun to investigate and validate many of these treatments, they have become accepted as effective

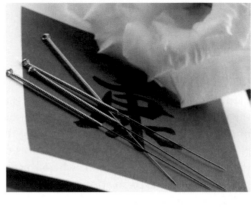

Based on traditional Chinese medicine, acupuncture is often helpful for pain relief.

options for both animals and humans. Alternative therapies are often used to complement traditional veterinary care.

## ACUPUNCTURE

In acupuncture, needles are inserted into identified points on the body to stimulate the body's immune system and promote healing. Based on traditional Chinese medicine, acupuncture is often helpful for pain relief.

## CHIROPRACTIC

A chiropractor adjusts the spinal vertebrae manually to relieve pressure and pain. Chiropractic treatments realign the spine and also help relieve pinched nerves, muscle weakness, and joint pain.

## HOLISTIC THERAPIES

Holistic medicine emphasizes the use of natural substances rather than pharmaceutical, surgical, or other conventional medical treatments. Practitioners use herbs, homeopathic remedies, and natural supplements to promote healing. Veterinarians often use holistic treatment in conjunction with traditional medicine, particularly for chronic conditions like arthritis and allergies. Tell your veterinarian about any holistic cures you are giving your dog so that she can integrate their effects into his overall treatment plan.

## TTOUCH

Tellington Touch, named for Linda Tellington-Jones, who developed the method, is a technique in which the practitioner releases tension and increases body awareness by using circular motions with her fingertips and hand pressure.

TTouch stimulates the nervous system and improves circulation. It is often used to help animals who are aggressive, fearful, or in pain.

## FIRST AID

Labs are such active dogs, there's a good chance yours will suffer an injury or other crisis at some point. Although you can't anticipate everything, here are some basics so that you'll be better prepared in an emergency. Once you have performed first aid, take your dog to the veterinarian immediately. Life-threatening consequences might not show up until later.

A frightened dog who is in a lot of pain, even your own beloved Labrador, may bite. If necessary, fashion a muzzle with a strip of cloth or gauze.

### BLEEDING

If blood is spraying from a wound, it may indicate a bleeding artery, which causes major blood loss. Slower blood loss indicates bleeding from a vein, which is easier to stop. Apply direct pressure to the wound with a piece of clean material. If that piece becomes saturated, add another one; don't remove the first one because you may dislodge a clot that is forming. You can also apply pressure just above the wound. If the wound continues to bleed, apply a pressure bandage but don't wrap it too tightly. If the injury is to a leg, elevate it above the level of the heart while applying pressure.

### BROKEN BONES

Keep your dog as still as possible while you stabilize the fracture. A rolled-up newspaper or magazine makes a good splint for a broken leg. Wrap the splinted leg with tape or cloth. Don't wrap too tightly or disturb the bones; repositioning could worsen the fracture. Transport the dog to the vet on a board, keeping him as immobilized as possible.

## PUPPY POINTER

Take precautions when socializing a young puppy who hasn't had his full series of vaccinations. Visitors should take off their shoes and wash their hands when coming into your house. Also, your puppy shouldn't be exposed to dogs with an unknown vaccine history. If you take him outside the home, don't put him on the ground where he might be exposed to dangerous diseases.

If your Lab's outside, watch him for signs of heatstroke, including excessive panting, pounding fast pulse, and excessive salivation.

## CHOKING

Labs who love to chew are at risk for swallowing tennis balls, squeakers, rawhides, rocks, and sticks. Signs of choking include struggling to breathe, gasping, panicking, and the gums turning blue or white. First try to sweep out the dog's mouth with your finger. Pull the tongue forward and remove any foreign material or vomit. Then hold his rear legs up (like a wheelbarrow) with his head down to dislodge the object.

If this doesn't work, use a modified Heimlich maneuver. With the dog standing, put your arms around him from behind and close your hands together to make a fist. Compress the abdomen sharply by pushing up with your fists at least five times. If this doesn't dislodge the object, administer a sharp blow to the back between the shoulder blades with the flat of your hand, then repeat the abdominal compressions until you are successful.

## FOOTPAD WOUNDS

If your Lab cuts his paw pad, even a small wound will bleed profusely. Check for a foreign object such as a thorn or piece of glass. Wash the area well; running water from a garden hose flushes a wound nicely. Dry thoroughly, then wrap the paw with gauze and tape it into place. Over the bandage, wrap the foot up to the ankle with an elastic self-stick bandage (Vet Wrap). Don't wrap so tightly that you cut off his circulation. If the wound looks deep, take your Lab to the vet. Otherwise, change the bandage within 24 hours and reassess.

## HEATSTROKE

It doesn't have to be hot for your dog to suffer from heatstroke. He'll run until he literally drops dead, so watch for these signs of heatstroke: excessive panting, bright red gums or gums that are too white, pounding fast pulse, excessive salivation, or the dog stopping and lying down, reluctant to continue.

To relieve heat exhaustion, wet his paws, head, abdomen, and chest to lower his body temperature. Take the dog to the vet, even if he appears to recover. Some of the consequences of heatstroke, like kidney failure, may not show up for days.

## POISON

If your dog has ingested snail bait, a poisonous plant, or other toxin, call the National Animal Poison Control Center for instructions (888-426-4435). Try to have the package or item in front of you when you call. Don't induce vomiting or give him anything to drink until you have consulted with Poison Control or a veterinarian.

## SNAKEBITE

A curious Lab may find himself nose to nose with a poisonous snake. If your dog gets bitten, do not use a tourniquet or try to suck out the venom. Keep him as still as possible to slow the spread of the venom and take him to the vet immediately. If you live in an area that has poisonous snakes, consider snake avoidance training for your dog.

## WOUND WITH PROTRUDING OBJECT

Leave it to a Labrador to get impaled by a stick. If this happens, do not remove the object. Secure it in place with gauze or other material to keep it from moving around. Wrap the area on both sides of the object to hold it in place without cutting off breathing or circulation. If the object is embedded in his side, wrap completely around the body. Transport your dog to the vet immediately on a flat board without allowing any more movement than absolutely necessary.

## THE SENIOR LAB

When your canine friend has a graying muzzle and his eyes are a little hazy, Labby has reached his golden years. A Lab is considered senior at 7 to 8 years of age, although many Labs hunt and compete until 11 or 12. Years of hard exercise will take their toll on your dog's joints, and he may move stiffly or have trouble standing up. His cognitive functions will slow down too. Schedule a senior health exam so that your vet can establish a baseline record for various health indicators.

To keep your elderly Labrador more comfortable:

A Lab is considered a senior at seven to eight years of age.

- Switch to a senior food that is lower in calories. Many senior foods also include joint supplements.
- Labby may have trouble walking on slick floors. A carpet runner or throw rug between rooms will help him get around.
- Let him out more often, as his bladder and bowel control will not be as reliable.
- Provide a heated or orthopedic bed.
- Moisten his food or add canned to make his meals more appetizing. As his sense of smell lessens, he may not be as interested in eating.
- Gentle walks will exercise his joints and keep him agile.
- Your Lab's vision and hearing are deteriorating, so have patience if he is slow responding to your call. A dog whose senses have dimmed may stand and bark, searching for his people. Labby could sometimes appear confused or disoriented, even in familiar places, as his mental faculties also slow down.
- Dental and gum disease can spread infection to the rest of the body, so regular teeth brushing and cleaning are especially important.

An older Lab is susceptible to a number of ailments:

## ARTHRITIS

Arthritis in Labradors is usually caused by other diseases, like hip and elbow dysplasia. If your Lab suffered a torn cruciate ligament or a broken bone, he is also likely to develop arthritis. Vets prescribe nonsteroidal anti-inflammatory drugs (NSAIDs) to relieve discomfort. Mild exercise, such as swimming, and supplements, like glucosamine and chondroitin, help keep aging joints flexible and improve mobility.

## CANCER

Rare compared to other breeds, cancer in Labs usually develops late in life. Mast cell tumors (a type of skin cancer that causes internal bleeding, gastric ulcers, and allergic reactions) are the most common. Treatment includes surgery followed by radiation. Veterinarians remove wide margins around the tumor to ensure that they eliminate all of the invasive cancerous cells.

## CATARACTS

When an elderly dog's eyes start to look bluish or gray, it may indicate cataracts, which are opaque spots on the lens of the eye. The disease causes inflammation that permanently damages the eye and may ultimately cause blindness unless surgically removed.

## LARYNGEAL PARALYSIS

This condition is part of a progressive neuromuscular disease that prevents the vocal folds on the sides of the larynx from opening and closing properly. The disorder makes breathing difficult; owners notice that their dog's bark sounds different, he pants excessively, and he recovers slowly from exercise. In severe cases, the condition is life threatening because the dog doesn't get enough air. To correct the problem, a surgeon must attach one or both vocal folds to the side of the larynx so that the dog can breathe. There is a risk after surgery that a dog will aspirate (inhale) food into the lungs, which causes pneumonia.

## LIPOMA

Many senior Labs get fatty tumors, called lipomas. They can appear anywhere on the body. To confirm the diagnosis, your vet will extract cells from the lump and examine them under a microscope. Because they aren't malignant, surgery isn't necessary unless the lipoma interferes with the dog's movement or comfort in some way.

# TRAINING YOUR
# LABRADOR RETRIEVER

Dogs thrive on a regular routine and want to know what is expected of them.

Labs are smart, eager to please, and love nothing better than working at your side. Originally developed to work next to a hunter and retrieve a fallen bird on command, this legacy of cooperation makes the Labrador one of the most trainable breeds.

## WHY TRAIN YOUR LABRADOR?

Dogs thrive on a regular routine and want to know what is expected of them. An untrained dog has no rules to live by, no daily schedule to count on, and no one to be his pack leader. Once trained, your dog will feel confident and secure about his place in the household, and he'll be less likely to develop problem behaviors due to confusion and lack of discipline. Plus, you'll have the tools to deal with problems when they occur.

A Lab doesn't mature until about three years of age, and without training you'll have a hyperactive 70-pound (31.8-kg) puppy on your hands. He'll drag you down the street, dig, chew, jump on strangers, and create chaos wherever he goes. You won't want to take him with you anywhere, and he'll be too wild to spend time in the house. The less time he spends with you, the worse he will behave.

A trained Lab, on the other hand, will have the skills to settle down and lie quietly at your feet. He'll sleep in the bedroom with the kids and accompany you on family vacations. Labby will be in the middle of the fun on Christmas morning. He'll be a pleasure to take on walks and will interact well with other dogs and people. In short, he'll be the perfect pet.

Obedience training develops a vocabulary you can use to communicate with each other. A dog isn't born knowing *sit*, *down*, and *come*. He needs to know that he's done something right, as well as when he's made a mistake. Once you understand how to train and your dog understands how to learn, you'll progress quickly and build a strong bond.

You may not think you've started training, but your new Lab is learning from the minute he walks in the door. He's watching you and learning what the rules are, what he can get away with, where he should (and shouldn't) relieve himself, and what the daily schedule is going to be. He's soaking up a lot of information, so guide him from the start.

## POSITIVE TRAINING

Most Labs are easily motivated by food and games, which makes training a lot of fun. Positive training methods will help your dog grow up into an enthusiastic, happy worker who listens to you and aims to please. Although this breed may seem tough and hardheaded, a Lab can actually be quite sensitive. Harsh training methods could make him overly shy or cause him to lash out aggressively in fear—something no Lab should ever do.

### WHAT ARE POSITIVE METHODS AND WHY DO THEY WORK?

Dog training has undergone a revolution over the past 20 years. Obedience class instructors used to drill owners on how to harshly punish dogs for making a mistake. We learned to yank on our dogs' collars and yell "No!" every time they did something wrong. We weren't having much fun, and our dogs were suffering.

Today's methods are much more humane and successful. Owners learn to teach their dogs the behaviors they want, rather than just punish the behaviors they don't like. We use praise and treats to provide positive reinforcement—in other words, catch the dog doing something right and reward him. The dog is motivated to repeat the behavior to earn more of his favorite things. Eventually, we phase out use of the treats every time and use praise (and still treats at times) as well.

### HOW DO YOU CORRECT A DOG WHO HAS DONE SOMETHING WRONG?

Anything you do to make the dog less likely to repeat a behavior is defined as a correction, or punishment. Harsh physical punishment is never acceptable—

you don't have to hit or otherwise hurt a Lab. If you feel that you can't get your dog to comply without strong physical methods, it's time to find a trainer and get some help. (See section "Finding a Professional Trainer.")

Labs will be Labs, however, and at some point in training, yours will test you to see if he can get away with disobeying. This is part of his natural learning curve, and you will have to muster up

Positive training methods will help your dog grow up into an enthusiastic, happy worker who listens to you and aims to please.

some patience and continue training. If you give up, your dog will learn that he'll eventually win and not have to do whatever you are asking. It's like a slot machine: Once he hits the jackpot, he'll keep trying to see if it will pay off again.

It takes six to eight weeks to turn a newly learned behavior into a habit. There is often a "learning plateau" at four to five weeks into the process, where he'll act like he's forgotten everything. Just keep at it, and he'll eventually get back on track.

When training, first be certain that your dog understands what you are asking of him. If he knows a command and doesn't do it, here are some of the methods you can use to correct him:

- **Verbal correction:** "No!" or "Ack!" using a harsh tone of voice. Your Lab will interpret your tone of voice and body language, even if he doesn't understand the words you are saying.
- **Withhold praise, petting, or treats:** Ignore your dog and refuse to make eye contact.
- **Walk away:** End the session.
- **Time-out:** Put him in his crate for five minutes.

Equally important as a correction is telling your dog when he's done something right. Again, your body language and tone of voice will help him interpret the meaning of what you say. Don't be afraid to act silly and use a high-pitched voice to convey your approval. He'll understand and be quicker to respond next time.

## SOCIALIZATION

Expose your Lab to as many experiences as possible so that he will grow up to be an emotionally healthy adult dog who is not overly fearful in new situations. A well-socialized dog has seen a lot of people, places, and things and has learned that they won't hurt him. Ideally, you'll start socializing your puppy when he is between 7 and 12 weeks old, when every new experience—good or bad—leaves a lasting impression, sometimes for the rest of his life. Some people bring their Lab home from the breeder, and the pup never leaves the yard or sees another dog until he begins obedience class months later. These dogs have to do a lot of catching up on their social skills.

## WHY SOCIALIZE?

A puppy kept isolated from other puppies will not learn his dog manners and will have trouble interacting with dogs appropriately when he finally meets them. That's why puppy kindergarten classes are so beneficial. The other puppies will teach him not to bite too hard or play too roughly. He'll be in a controlled environment where all the puppies are required to be current on their vaccines and an experienced instructor will guide their play sessions.

When training, first be certain that your dog understands what you are asking of him.

## HOW TO SOCIALIZE YOUR LAB

If you have a new adult dog, it's never too late to start introducing him to the world. If Labby has had scary experiences (or no experiences at all) when he was younger, he'll act shyly or fearfully in new situations.

Whether puppy or adult, your dog needs to meet and be handled by people of all ages, shapes, colors, and sizes, as well as by people wearing raincoats, uniforms, floppy hats, or carrying umbrellas. People on bikes, on skateboards, and riding

When I volunteered for Labrador Retriever rescue, I brought an adult Lab home from the shelter who promptly ran straight into a picture window; he'd never been close enough to a house to understand what glass was. Another foster dog tried to walk across the pool and fell in. He didn't realize that he couldn't walk on water because he'd never seen a pool before. These two incidents illustrate how important socialization is!

in wheelchairs or strollers—all are new and scary to an unsocialized dog. Besides animals and people, introduce him to objects he hasn't seen before: cars, lawnmowers, dishwashers, and other potentially scary things.

Imagine Labby the first time he sees an umbrella. You wouldn't just walk up to him and explode it open in his face. He'd be afraid of umbrellas for the rest of his life. Put an open umbrella on the floor and let him sneak up on it, sniff it, and decide it won't hurt him. Then move it a little, pick it up, and hold it over your head. Close and gently reopen the umbrella. Leave the room with it and bring it back in with you. Carry an open umbrella with you while you go for a walk together. Have someone else handle the umbrella. Be sure that he sees umbrellas in different places, indoors and out. In conjunction with lots of treats and happy praise, he'll decide that an umbrella is a very good thing.

Plan your Lab's outings so that he has positive experiences. Don't force him to approach someone or something he is afraid of, but don't comfort him either. He may misinterpret your worried tone and decide there is good reason to be scared. How you react will help him learn that there is nothing to be afraid of. Start at a distance where he feels safe, and talk to him in a happy voice. Move closer, as long as he's comfortable, and back off a little if he appears frightened, without making a big deal of it.

## CRATE TRAINING

You may cringe at the idea of putting your beloved Labrador in a "cage," but if introduced correctly, dogs consider the crate their den and will often seek it out as a safe place to rest.

### WHY USE A CRATE?

There are many good reasons to crate train your Lab. A crate is an effective alternative until you feel that you can safely leave him alone unsupervised. A dog alone loose in the house or yard feels that he has to react to everything he hears or sees. That's a lot of responsibility. He'll resort to chewing, barking, or other problem behaviors to relieve his stress. Once he's in the crate, he'll feel secure and relax.

If your Lab is in his crate, he won't jump on visitors or run out the front door when people arrive. When you travel, he will feel safe in his familiar crate when in a hotel room or on an airplane. If you are in a car accident, he won't get thrown out or lost. A stay at the vet's office will also be less stressful if he's used to being confined.

Additionally, a crate is an excellent housetraining aid. Because a dog doesn't want to soil where he sleeps, he will learn to hold it until you let him out.

Your Lab should never be left alone in the crate all day while you are at work and then be expected to sleep in it all night. Have someone come in to let him out every few hours to relieve himself and get some exercise.

## HOW TO CRATE TRAIN YOUR LAB

To begin crate training your Lab, toss in a treat and let him eat it with the door open. Do this several times throughout the day. Next put his dinner bowl in the crate with the door open. Over the course of a few meals, move the food bowl in, toward the back of the crate. Eventually your Lab should be completely in the crate with the door open while he eats.

Whether puppy or adult, your dog needs to meet and be handled by people and introduced to new situations.

When he appears comfortable, shut the door while he is eating. Leave it shut for a few seconds. Gradually increase the amount of time the door is shut. Once he is able to stay in the crate until his meal is finished, put him inside at random times for a few minutes while you sit nearby. Give your Lab a special chewy that he only gets at crate time.

He may whine and scratch at first. Ignore him. If he barks, just rap on the crate to interrupt him but don't say anything. If you speak to him or let him out, you are rewarding him with attention. When he stops and settles down for a few seconds, praise him in a happy voice, give him a few treats, and let him out. Be sure that he gets the treats while he is still in the crate so that he associates being in the crate with good things.

Gradually increase the time your Lab stays in the crate. Leave the room and come back without acknowledging him. Pretty soon he'll settle down and take a nap without making a fuss.

## HOUSETRAINING

Teach your dog not to eliminate in the house. A puppy doesn't have bladder or bowel control and must learn to "hold it" until he is in an appropriate place. An adult dog who has lived outside has never regulated his urge to relieve himself. At any age, Labs are easy to housetrain and quickly learn the rules. Puppies need a little more time to develop control, but they are usually reliable by four months of age.

### HOW TO HOUSETRAIN

If your Lab is new to your home, start housetraining the day he arrives. The routine is the same for adult dogs and puppies, except that puppies will have to go out more often.

Dogs thrive on a regular schedule. At a minimum, take your Lab out as soon as he gets up in the morning, immediately after breakfast, before you leave for work, when you get home, after playtime or a nap, after dinner, and before bedtime. If you have another dog, take them out together. He will learn by example and will want to go where the other dog urinates.

Feed at regular times, and pick up the food after 20 minutes. Free-feeding makes it harder to regulate his need for breaks. Remove water and food by 8 p.m. so that he'll be able to make it through the night without an accident.

After he eats, eliminates, and has had some free time, put your Lab in his crate for an hour or so. Then take him out for another potty break. Choose an area where you would like him to go. He'll recognize the odors when you take him to the same spot each time. This is not the time to play a game or talk to him; he'll forget the purpose of the excursion. When he urinates, praise him and give a treat. Pick a word to use while he goes, like "potty" or "hurry." If he doesn't eliminate on his outing, put him back in the crate immediately. Once reliably housetrained, you won't have to go with Labby every time. For now, he needs your praise to show him what is right.

When you bring him in, give him about 30 minutes loose in the house. Then put him on a leash at your side or back in his crate. Confining him in this way teaches him to hold it. Wait about an hour and take him out again. He'll soon learn that going outside means going potty, getting a treat, and best of all, coming back into the house with you.

Once you feel comfortable giving him some freedom, watch for signs he needs to go out. Dogs and puppies will walk in circles, sniffing until they find just the right spot. An adult male may line up with the corner of a couch or wall. If he starts to pee, interrupt him with a loud "No!" and take him out. If he doesn't go while he's outside, crate him for an hour and try again.

## HOUSETRAINING ACCIDENTS

If your Lab has an accident, try to catch him in the act or he won't understand what all the fuss is about. Say "No!" and quickly take him outside to relieve himself. At first he may think that you aren't supposed to see him eliminate,

The housetraining routine is the same for adult dogs and puppies, except that puppies will have to go out more often.

not that doing it in the house is wrong, so he'll try to go to another room. Rubbing his nose in it or hitting him with a rolled-up newspaper accomplishes nothing. He'll just learn to be afraid of you.

Males, especially unneutered ones, will lift their leg to mark territory. Treat marking like you would any accident: Catch him in the act and correct him. Some dogs suffer from spay incontinence or a urinary tract infection. Both are easily treated, so see your vet if a housetrained dog suddenly can't hold it.

Remove odors from accidents with a specially formulated stain and odor remover. Once a dog has urinated on a particular spot, he'll return to the same place over and over unless you eliminate every trace of urine. Our dogs have a much better sense of smell than we do, and water or other household cleaners don't remove the odor completely.

## THE BASIC COMMANDS

When teaching an obedience command, think of it as a three-part sequence: 1. You give a command; 2. the dog performs; 3. he gets a reward (treats, petting, or a game). Figure out what your dog loves most and incorporate that into his reward. He will respond quickly and even offer the behavior when you didn't ask for it in hopes of earning the prize. When he is responding reliably every time, randomly reward him: every other time, every fourth time, etc., on an unpredictable schedule. Occasionally give him a jackpot—extra treats or a great toy or game—when he responds really well. If his performance drops off, increase the reward frequency, then back off again. Always give him verbal praise for a job well done.

Once your dog understands a command, he must generalize his learning. His mental picture of *sit* may mean that he's in the backyard and that you are holding the leash and are standing in front of him with the treat bag in your hand. He doesn't know *sit* in the driveway, at the vet's office, when your spouse says "Sit," or when you are sitting in a chair. He needs to relearn the behavior in assorted situations before he understands the command thoroughly.

## PUPPY POINTER

Young puppies cannot go eight hours without a potty break. If you are gone all day at work, hire a dog walker to come in at midday so that Labby has a chance to eliminate.

Teach the *sit* by luring your Lab into position and then rewarding him with a treat.

Don't let all your hard work go to waste. Use the following commands every day so that your Labrador won't forget them.

## SIT

*Sit* is the easiest and usually the first thing we teach our dogs. *Sit* is also a practical command. Ask your dog to sit when you want him to settle down, before you attach a leash, while you groom him, before you put down his food bowl, before you throw the ball, and when he meets people. There are an endless number of opportunities to use the *sit* every day.

### How to Teach *Sit*

Teach the *sit* by luring Labby into position. Hold a treat in your hand above his head, just barely out of reach. You don't want him to jump up. Slowly move your hand backward over his head, and he should sit to reach it. Don't try to push his butt to the ground—his instinct will be to resist and push back up. As soon as his rear touches the ground, praise him enthusiastically and deliver the treat. Release him with an "Okay" or similar word that tells him the exercise is over. By the third or fourth try, he'll anticipate your signal and start to sit as soon as you raise your hand. Keep it fun and quit when you get a small success.

Now it's time to marry the word "sit" with the action. As your dog starts to sit, say the command. When he sits, reward and release him. After a number of repetitions, he will respond to the word "sit" and you won't have to show him a treat or use a hand motion.

## STAY

Once your Lab knows the *sit* exercise, start to teach the *stay*, a command that tells your Lab to stay put until you tell him it's okay to get up.

## How to Teach *Stay*

When you first taught the *sit*, as soon as his rear touched the floor, you gave him a treat and released him. Now delay for just a second or two, and before he starts to get up, beat him to it: Reward and release him. Gradually lengthen the time before he gets the reward and release. Then vary the length of time: 10 seconds, 30 seconds, 5 seconds, etc. Once he is staying, add the *stay* command. The hand signal for this is

Teaching basic training will result in a well-mannered dog.

your open palm raised in front of his nose. He'll soon learn to respond to the hand command.

Body language is important. If you tower over your dog, he'll be intimidated and may shrink away. If you bend over toward him, this will invite him to get up and come to you. Stand naturally a step or two away.

Be consistent, and always release your Lab in the same way. Go back, touch him, and say "Okay" so that there is no doubt in his mind as to when he can get up. Otherwise, he will be watching your body language for clues and get confused.

Once he is doing a solid *stay* for one minute with you right in front of him, go back to short *stays* and gradually move farther away. Practice random distances, and once he is good at that, you can add random lengths of time.

When your Lab breaks the *stay* (and he will—it is part of the learning process), you'll see him getting restless and then start to stand. Try to stop him with a loud "No!" before he gets all the way up. He'll learn to settle and stay put. If he gets up, put him back without a word. Take him all the way back to where you asked him to stay originally. Remain closer to him on the next try.

The next step is to add distractions. This is where his obedience training becomes useful in everyday life. Practice *stays* (on leash) at the pet supply store, in the park, while on walks, and with kids throwing balls nearby. Go back to short *stays* with you close to him before you move up to harder distractions. He won't initially understand that he has to stay when there is a lot going on around him. Practice makes perfect!

## DOWN

The *down* exercise is another useful skill. At home, your dog can lie down at your feet while you work, when you have visitors, and while you groom him. Away from home, a *down* helps Labby mind his manners in the waiting room, at the vet's office, or other public places.

People often find it harder to teach the *down* exercise. It is physically more awkward for the trainer to lure the dog into a *down*, and your Lab may resist being in a submissive position.

### How to Teach *Down*

Armed with treats, kneel down next to him and ask him to sit. While holding the treat in front of his nose, pull it down to the ground and then away. Position the treat between his feet as he lowers himself. As you slowly pull it away, he'll follow his nose to the ground and stretch out into a *down*.

Use a happy tone of voice when you call your dog, and always give him a reason to be glad that he came when you asked him to.

Even though young dogs have lots of energy and learn quickly, they don't have a lot of endurance or much of an attention span. Training sessions should be short and fun, less than five minutes at a time, so that puppies don't get bored.

What you are looking for are your Lab's front elbows touching the floor. Many dogs will crouch with their butts in the air and bounce right back up, but that's not a *down*. Once he is correctly in position, hold the treat at ground level and move it in toward him so that he isn't lured out of position. This may take numerous tries!

For puppies, kneel on the ground with one knee raised and lure him under your leg. He'll have to go down to get the treat on the other side. Again, lure him into the correct position with a treat.

Always end the session after your dog has done something right, even if you have to take a few steps backward in his training.

## COME (RECALL)

*Come* is a command that could save your dog's life. A reliable *recall* is essential if you are ever going to let your Lab off leash in public, even at the dog park. Don't wait until he runs into the street after the neighbor's cat to teach this vital skill. Practice regularly in different situations and with distractions to keep the *recall* fresh in his mind and reliable.

Always give your dog a reason to be glad he came when called. If you call and then yell at him for coming slowly, you have punished him for obeying you. If you must give him medicine or something else he doesn't like, go get him. Or reward him for coming with treats or a game, then move on to the less pleasant activity.

### How to Teach *Come*

Use a happy tone of voice when you call your dog. You will intimidate him if you stand stiff as a board and issue a strict *come* command. If you say "Come here!" your voice will naturally lift a little at the end and sound friendly. Praise him the second he looks your way. Jump up and down, cheer him on, and act like he's the smartest dog in the world. If he's reluctant, crouch down and open your arms. This is an open invitation to play, and he should make a beeline to you. As soon as he arrives, reward him; then let him go. Yes, I said let him go. He gets to continue having fun, which is a reward in itself.

Play relay games with family members and friends. Have one person call Labby and reward him with a treat. The next person should do the same thing, and so on. When someone else calls the dog, stand still and ignore him. A treat every time might get boring, so use different rewards for coming. Throw a tennis ball or toy. Turn around and run, and he'll love to chase you. Roll on the ground and roughhouse for a few seconds. Figure out what your dog likes and reward him with it.

There will come a point in his *recall* training when your dog will test you and refuse to come. Put him on a long line so that you can enforce the command and reel him in. You never want to call a dog if you can't make him comply. If he learns that he doesn't have to come when called, you'll have a lot of retraining to do.

## HEEL (WALK NICELY ON LEASH)

Does your Lab drag you down the street? If so, it's time to dedicate your daily walks to training. In the beginning, you may not get much of a walk, but if you work with him a few minutes, then let him haul you off for the rest of the walk, you've accomplished nothing.

The *heel* position is one in which your Lab is at your side, his ear lined up with the side seam of your pants. Ideally, he should stay there, or close to it, when you are walking together. He shouldn't be allowed to take a single step while pulling.

### How to Teach *Heel*

Ask your dog to sit before you open the door and remain sitting until you let him go out; then, make him *walk* out, not blast off. It will usually take about three tries before he'll start to understand what you are teaching. Go slowly and start over if he charges out.

Once you are finally on your way, your dog should be more attentive because you are asking him to do things your way and rewarding him when he does.

Take a step or two. If he is still at your side, give a treat and praise him. Keep up this routine for several feet (m), then break and relax a minute. Start again and practice some more. After a day or two, you may be able to take

Attending a training class will help your dog become better socialized and keep you on track with your training schedule.

five steps before your Lab starts to pull. Try to anticipate when he is going to lunge ahead. Stop and praise him before he gets a chance to make a mistake. Vary how many steps you take before you stop to feed and praise him: two steps, five, one, ten, etc. This random reward system will keep him thinking and will make him work harder to get it right and earn that treat.

When he makes a mistake by lunging, stop walking and just stand there until he looks back at you, or you can try suddenly changing directions. Praise him as he comes back to the *heel* position, and start over. If he really gets obnoxious, quit for the day. Bring him in and put him in his crate without saying anything. You just ended all the fun, and he doesn't want that. This is often punishment enough, and he'll remember it. If you are getting frustrated, quit. Try to end on a high note when he has done something right, even if it is just a *sit*.

At first, he will not do as well out in public, where there are so many things to look at, so be prepared to reward him for smaller successes. As he learns what you expect of him, he will improve.

# FINDING A PROFESSIONAL TRAINER

All Lab owners should attend obedience classes, even if you've owned a dog before. Besides training your dog, he'll get social contact and practice with distractions outside the home. Attending class will keep you on track with your training schedule, and you'll have help from a professional to guide your efforts.

With that in mind, how do you find a good trainer? Anyone can call herself a trainer, so you need to look further than a business card to see if the classes are right for you and your Lab.

Ask for recommendations from:

- other Lab owners or your breeder
- your veterinarian
- local obedience clubs or humane society
- parks and recreation department in your city
- national associations, such as the Association of Pet Dog Trainers (APDT) at www.apdt.com and the International Association of Canine Professionals (IACP) at http://canineprofessionals.com

Evaluate potential instructors by asking yourself the following questions:

- Is the trainer a member of any local obedience clubs or national associations?
- How long has this person been training dogs professionally?
- Does she have experience with Labs? What breed does the instructor own? If the trainer has only owned toy breeds, where has she gotten experience handling large dogs?
- Can you audit a class session? If so, are the students having fun? Are they successful? Do you like the training methods and general atmosphere?
- What is the ratio of students to instructors? Are there assistants? Do students get individual attention?
- Are continuing classes available? Private lessons?

Invest a few months of effort when you first get your Lab, and it will pay off with years of enjoyment. Training your Lab takes time and effort, but you'll build a better relationship with him and avoid a lot of the issues that are described in the next chapter, which covers problem behaviors.

# CHAPTER 8

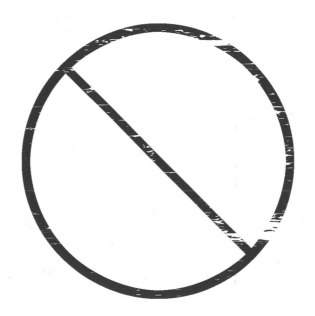

# SOLVING PROBLEMS WITH YOUR LABRADOR RETRIEVER

Rigorous exercise will help your Lab calm down so that he won't redirect his excess energy to destroying your belongings.

While dogs just do what comes naturally, some of their activities are not acceptable to us. And that is when those natural behaviors—like barking, chewing, and digging—are labeled problems. Even a well-trained Lab will push the limits of your patience during his boisterous teenage years. He won't automatically grow out of it, so you must put some effort into dealing with these problems. Here are some methods to help minimize problem behaviors in general:

- **Management:** It may be easier to manage your Lab's environment than to prevent unwanted behaviors. Crate or confine him when you can't supervise. Pick up things he might chew. Build a solid fence so that he can't bark at the neighbors.
- **Basic obedience training:** *Sit*, *stay*, and *down* may appear to have nothing to do with behavior issues, but problems sometimes disappear completely after a few weeks of classes. Why? Training gives him the structure and discipline he needs to feel secure in his place in the world, and issues are often resolved without further measures.
- **A regular schedule:** A dog is less likely to misbehave if he can count on a daily routine. Establish a schedule for meals, outings, playtime, and bedtime. If your Lab has issues and you can't make it home at your usual time, have a dog walker visit and take him out.
- **Exercise:** Trainer Job Michael Evans once wrote, "A tired dog is a good dog." Rigorous exercise helps a Lab calm down so that he won't redirect his excess

energy to destroying the couch. Walks, games of fetch, obedience classes, and sports (like agility) will wear him out so that he's ready to relax when it's time to settle down.

- **Mental games:** Hide-and-seek, tricks, find the toy, fetch, and puzzle toys will exercise your dog's mind while relieving boredom and anxiety. Give him a treat-dispensing ball or toy when he has to be alone. Fill it with a mix of kibble and some extra-tasty treats. He'll stay occupied and won't need to make up his own fun.
- **Let your Lab live indoors:** An outdoor-only Lab is lonely and isolated and will act out his unhappiness by misbehaving. Let him sleep indoors with you too. It is time spent with his pack and therefore reassuring to him.
- **Hire a dog walker:** If you work long hours, have a dog walker take him out every day or take him to doggy day care several times a week to help relieve boredom and burn off some of his excess energy.

Ask your entire family to help you train Labby. Once he realizes that everyone knows the rules, he'll give up his wild ways.

## BARKING

It's unreasonable to expect your Lab never to bark at all. It's a natural behavior and occasionally you may even want him to bark. But first you must figure

# Dog Tale

When we built a dog run on our 5-acre property, we made a strategic error in our plans. Built so that it overlooked the house, the run also had a view of the driveway and street, so the dogs could see anyone and everything that went by. Labs have a loud, distinctive voice, and our dogs' barking carried over to the neighbor's house far too well. After a few complaints, we decided to try a bark control device that you hang on the fence. Every time a dog barks, it emits a shrill beep that interrupts the dog and supposedly makes him stop barking. The problem was that people could hear the sound too. And when one dog barked, they all got corrected by the beep, so they didn't associate the correction with their own barking. One day I got a call from the neighbor: "What is that horrible beeping noise coming from your house? It's worse than the barking!" We hadn't realized the beep carried that far. Needless to say, we got rid of that so-called solution. Instead, we planted a hedge to block the dogs' view of the street.

out why he's barking in order to stop him. Whatever the reason, you owe it to your neighbors to get your dog's barking under control.

Some Labs are chronic barkers and some aren't. Labs aren't really guard dogs, but all dogs sound the alarm if someone enters their territory. Look at barking from a dog's point of view. Every time someone walks by the house, he barks and they leave. The mail carrier or delivery person arrives, Labby barks, and she leaves. Because barking gets results, it quickly becomes a habit. In your dog's mind, he's doing a great job chasing off all of these intruders, so barking is self-rewarding.

Another reason a dog barks is because he's spoiled or bossy. Think of the last time your Lab dropped a tennis ball in your lap and stood looking at you, wagging his tail. You threw the ball and he kept coming back for more. If you tried to quit, he barked at you. He wanted something, and he was going to harangue you until he got it. Eventually you gave up and gave in. Gotcha. He just learned that barking got him what he wanted: a game of fetch. They don't call Labs relentless retrievers for nothing.

## HOW TO MANAGE IT

Negative attention is better than no attention at all in your Lab's eyes, so try not to reward him with attention when he's barking. Instead, reward him when he's quiet. Make him sit before you throw that tennis ball, and he'll stop barking long enough so that you can reward him with a throw.

When the neighbors are having a party, bring your Lab indoors, away from the excitement. Close the drapes if he's barking out the front window. If he spends a lot of time barking in the yard, put up a solid fence so that he can't

# Dog Tale

Obedience dumbbells are made of wood, metal, or plastic and are used for retrieving exercises in competition. My dog Tank did not have a typical Lab's soft mouth. He mouthed the wooden dumbbell and wouldn't hold it still. We practiced endlessly and the bar of his dumbbell got pretty mangled. One day at a show, I left Tank on a *down-stay* by my chair while I talked to a friend nearby. When I turned back, his dumbbell was a pile of wood chips in front of him. I had to buy a new one before we went in the ring—but this time I bought plastic.

*Labs were bred to carry things in their mouths, so chewing is an instinctive behavior.*

see out. Yelling at him from the house is like joining in the barkathon. If you call him to you and put him in a crate, he just got punished for coming. He's not likely to come again so willingly. Go get him, bring him in, and crate him for a short time.

You can also interrupt the noise by banging together a couple of metal dishes or tossing a soda can with a bunch of pennies inside. You'll break up the action long enough to get your dog's attention and redirect it to some acceptable activity. If you don't give him something else to do, he'll just go back to barking.

Another thing you can do is put your Lab's barking on cue. When he's barking, praise him and give it a name, like "speak." It may not make sense because you are rewarding him for something you don't like, but you can then teach a *quiet* command by rewarding him the instant he stops. Name that behavior "quiet," "no speak," "zip it," or whatever you like, and now you can turn the barking off when you need to. The reward for being quiet needs to be better than the self-reinforcement he gets for barking.

## CHEWING

Owning a Lab means that the kids will finally learn to pick up their clothes. You'll never completely prevent Labs from chewing; they were bred to carry things in their mouths, so it is an instinctive behavior. The things I've seen them eat are endless, including car seat belts, screen doors, table legs, 2 x 4s (5.1 x 10.2 cm), buckets, blankets, dog beds, bushes, an air-conditioner unit, wood salad bowl, shoes, and a tube of cortisone cream. And that was just at my house. You don't want to pay for surgery to remove any of these tidbits from your Lab's gut, so invest some money in safe chew toys. You'll be glad you did!

Puppies explore the world with their mouths. They don't have hands, so they taste everything, and chewing these items is the next logical step. Once begun, destructive chewing can quickly turn into a habit that is hard to break because dogs enjoy it so much. Besides the fact that chewing is just plain fun, a dog 6 to 12 months old is losing his baby teeth, and his gums are sore as the new teeth begin to break through. Consequently, he chews to ease the pain.

Dogs sometimes chew for other reasons: loneliness, boredom, separation anxiety, or lack of exercise. Chewing is a Lab's way of redirecting his frustrations.

## HOW TO MANAGE IT

First, correct and redirect. If you catch your Labrador chewing something inappropriate, interrupt him and give him something he's allowed to gnaw on. When you aren't able to supervise a super chewer, put him in his crate with something he's allowed to chew.

Use products like a bitter apple spray to make targets like furniture legs and wire cords taste bad. You can also use red pepper sauce, although it might stain fabrics.

Also, dog-proof his environment. Pick up tempting items like shoes, clothes, patio chair pads, pillows, leashes, and children's toys. Close the doors to the laundry room and bedroom. Put a barrier around the flowerbeds until he learns to leave your plants alone.

When you give your Labrador a new item to chew, supervise. A Lab can destroy most squeaky toys, stuffed animals, rawhides, tennis balls, and rubber bones in just a few minutes. You don't want him swallowing indigestible pieces. When the item starts to fall apart, take it away. Some of my favorite Labrador chew toys include:

- **Galileo bones:** These super-hard rubber bones wear down but don't break up into large pieces that can be swallowed. It's the only bone I've found that lasts for up to a year.
- **Large woven rope toys:** As the strings come loose, they aren't large enough to cause a blockage. For a Lab who is teething, freeze the rope just like you would freeze a pacifier. When it gets shredded and starts to fall apart, throw it away. Big chunks of string will block his digestive tract.
- **Giant ice cubes:** In the summer, I make large popsicles for my dogs. I freeze a quart-size tub of water filled with dog biscuits, carrots, peanut butter, hot dog chunks, and other

**BE AWARE!**
Behavior that is not rewarded is not as likely to be repeated. Figure out what reward your Lab gets as a result of his actions, and if you can, remove it.

Dogs with problem behaviors like barking and chewing are often also diggers.

goodies. Then I dump it out on a tray and let them work on it for a few hours.

• **Wet washcloths:** A frozen wet washcloth makes a soothing pacifier for a dog who is teething and needs to chew. Take it away before he destroys it completely and swallows it.

## DIGGING

Dogs with problem behaviors like barking and chewing are often also diggers. The motivations are similar: boredom, loneliness, and anxiety. But there are a few other reasons to consider.

### HOW TO MANAGE IT

If your Lab is not spayed or neutered, he or she will do anything to escape the yard and breed when there is an unaltered dog nearby. Alter your Lab, or keep him or her indoors (preferably in a crate) when females are in heat.

Dogs find rodents hard to resist. If you have gophers or ground squirrels, get rid of these pests. Poisons can harm your dog, so be careful about what measures you use. Humane traps are effective and safer for your canine family member.

Dogs like to dig a hole under a bush to lie in and keep cool during hot weather. When it's hot, fill a kiddie pool in the yard so that Labby can cool off during the day. Raised dog beds made of PVC pipe and shade cloth allow air to circulate around your Lab and keep him cool. Place one in a shady spot where he has been digging.

When it is time to work in the garden, don't let your Lab see you dig. He'll be only too happy to help! Spray your plants and the surrounding soil with animal repellent, available at pet supply or garden stores. You can also put chicken wire or large rocks around the base of new plants.

Here are a few more solutions:

• Install a pet door so that your Lab can come and go as he pleases. This will relieve his anxiety when he is home alone and lessen his need to get into mischief.

- Bury his feces in the hole he has dug. Although this won't stop every dog, especially those who eat feces, the unpleasant smell is often an effective repellent.
- Run a strip of chicken wire or hardware cloth along the bottom of the fence and extend it out into the yard several inches (cm). Then cover it with soil or rocks.
- Establish a digging area for your Lab. Partially bury a few bones or other smelly treats to encourage him to dig there.

## HOUSE SOILING

Labs are unlikely to suddenly start having accidents in the house. If your Lab has previously been reliably housetrained, the first step is a trip to the veterinarian for a checkup to make sure there isn't a medical reason for the lapse in housetraining.

If your Lab is urinating in the house, there could be several different causes. Dogs of either sex can get urinary tract infections. If he has diarrhea, clean it up and take a sample with you to the vet's. Parasites or bloody mucus in the stool sample might indicate a condition that needs to be treated.

Females sometimes develop spay incontinence, which means that they leak urine, even while they sleep, and can't help it. Inexpensive medications manage the problem. Watch your Lab to see if she is licking herself a lot; she may be trying to ease the irritation from the urine coming in contact with her skin.

### HOW TO MANAGE IT

When medical reasons are eliminated, it is time to look at your Labrador's environment:

- Can your dog get outside often enough?
- Does he know how to tell you he needs to go out?
- Has something changed in the physical layout of your home or yard? Has a recent remodeling project confused him? Is there gravel or concrete where his favorite potty spot used to be?
- Is there a new dog or cat

The way to deal with an unexplained lapse in housetraining is to go back to the beginning and start the process over again, as if your Lab was still a puppy.

in the family? He may be marking to establish his territory. Females can mark too.

- Is there a new person in the household? Guests? Has someone moved out? Is there tension or a major upheaval in the family's life? Is he not getting as much attention as he used to? Your Lab may be stressed and confused by changes that have nothing to do with him.

- Is it raining or snowing? Even a water dog like a Lab doesn't want to go out in bad weather and get his feet wet.

Whatever the reason, the way to deal with an unexplained lapse is to go back to the beginning and start the housetraining process over again, as if he were still a puppy:

1. Establish a regular schedule of eating, playing, going to bed, and going potty.
2. Pick up water in the evening so that he doesn't drink right before bedtime.
3. Confine him when you can't supervise. Block doorways with baby gates or sheets of cardboard. Crate him at night and when you are gone.
4. Go out with him on every potty break, and praise him when he goes.
5. Catch him in the act if he has an accident, and take him outside. Clean up mistakes with odor-neutralizing cleaner so that the smell won't tempt him to go there again.

## JUMPING UP

A rude dog who leaps up and frightens people is an annoyance and a liability. When he slams you into the wall while planting giant paws on your shoulders, he wants your attention, to smell your breath so that he can identify you, and to lick your face like a puppy would to show submission.

### HOW TO MANAGE IT

Your Lab doesn't automatically know the proper way to greet people. If he's sitting, he can't jump, so teach him to sit every time he meets someone. Practice in different places and with lots of different people. Have your Labrador on a leash so that you can enforce your command by walking him away if he doesn't comply. Don't take him back to meet the person again until he sits for you. If you can't make him sit, don't ask for it because he'll know when he can ignore you. If you ever allow him to jump up with no correction of any kind, he'll assume that it is sometimes okay, and retraining takes longer.

Keep treats handy while your dog is learning so that you can reward a correct response. Praise him when he sits. Don't touch him or make eye contact because this will invite him right back up. You may think that you are correcting him, but if you touch him, even to push him away, he is being rewarded with attention. Don't let him get up until you say "Okay" or a similar release word.

**BE AWARE!**
When teaching your Lab not to jump on people, hang a leash on the doorknob at the front door so that you can hook him up before you open it.

Here are some more solutions:

- Step on the leash so that your Lab automatically corrects himself as he jumps up. Dogs always jump back up immediately, so be ready to do it again and again until he can sit for at least a few seconds.

- Fold your arms across your chest and don't even look at your dog; turn your back, ignore him, and walk away. If walking away just revs him up more, stand still and wait until he quits jumping. This may take a few minutes, but if he gets no response from you, eventually he'll give up, even if it's only for a second or two. Praise and give him some low-energy attention. Excited attention will make him jump up again.

- Wait a few minutes before you interact with Labby when you come home. Put your things down, get a drink, and then give him some attention. He's probably been asleep and needs to go outside, so let him have time to relieve himself. He'll quickly learn and not start bouncing off the walls when you come through the door.

- If he is acting wild when company comes, put him in a time-out in his crate until he settles down. Then let him out and hook up his leash so that you can stop him if he jumps on someone. Put him back in the crate multiple times if you have to.

- If you want your Lab to jump on you occasionally, teach him a word or phrase for it, like "paws up!" or "hug" while patting your chest in a friendly way. Then tell him "Off" and turn away so that he knows when to quit.

## NIPPING OR PLAY BITING

As I wrote earlier in this chapter, puppies explore the world with their mouths. When they play with their littermates, they bite and nip each other. But when a pup nips too hard, the other puppy disciplines him with a sharp bark and tells him to back off. The offended puppy often quits playing and goes off to find another littermate who plays nicely.

When a Lab bites at your hands, he thinks it is a game, just like the ones he played with his littermates. But even eight-week-old Labrador pups can deliver a painful bite. Teach your dog that it is never okay to put his mouth on you, whether he is young or full grown.

## HOW TO MANAGE IT

Imitate another dog when your Lab starts nipping. Give a loud yelp and turn away from him. Don't try to push him off you; touching is attention. Hands waving in the air are great fun and just invite him to play and nip more. Fold your arms against your body and stand still. You have ended the game. If he continues, put him in his crate until he calms down. Even small children can use this method effectively.

Another technique is that when he mouths you, quietly remove your hand and wait a few seconds. Snatching your hand away will encourage him to grab. As soon as you reach out to touch him, he'll probably nip again. Praise him quietly when he doesn't. By the third or fourth try, he'll start getting the idea.

Set your Lab up for success. Start by touching body parts where he is not so sensitive, then work up to touching spots where he is likely to react. Praise

Be sure to reward your dog when he performs a desired behavior.

him and deliver a treat when he allows you to touch his body and remains calm without mouthing.

## WHEN TO SEEK PROFESSIONAL HELP

Don't be shy about getting professional help with your Lab's problem behaviors. We aren't born knowing how to train dogs any more than we are born knowing how to fix cars.

Get help:

- when your attempts to fix a problem aren't working
- when your dog is too much for you to handle, either because of his strength or his wild behavior
- when your dog guards his food or toys and won't let you touch them, or he refuses to get off the couch or bed
- when your dog has snapped, growled, or shown other signs of aggression toward anyone at home or in public
- if you are afraid of your dog

## FINDING A PROFESSIONAL BEHAVIORIST

Consult with your trainer, but realize that not all trainers are qualified to work with problem dogs because they don't deal one on one with them very often. Your instructor may be able to refer you to a qualified expert. Fortunately, you have several options when searching for assistance.

A behavioral consultant will work with you to identify and deal with your dog's specific issues. The International Association of Animal Behavior Consultants (IAABC) (www.iaabc.org) certifies consultants and maintains a database on the Internet to help you locate a qualified individual.

The next step up the ladder of experts is an applied animal behaviorist. Certified by the Animal Behavior Society (ABS) (www.animalbehaviorsociety.

## PUPPY POINTER

When your Labrador puppy was a baby, you thought it was cute when he jumped up on you and barked when you came home. He was so happy to see you! Now that he weighs 75 pounds (34 kg), it's not so cute anymore. Even an eight-week-old puppy can learn to sit in front of you and wait to be petted.

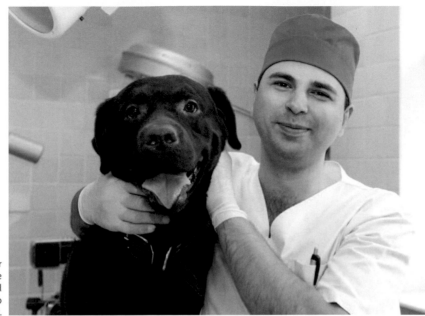

A problem behavior may actually be the result of a medical issue, so have your Lab checked by a vet.

org), an applied animal behaviorist has at least a master's degree in behavioral science and has studied biology, zoology, and related subjects. She will also have advanced skills in assessment, counseling, behavior modification, and intervention.

For another resource, ask your veterinarian or local veterinary specialty hospital for a referral to a veterinary behaviorist. These individuals have earned certification from the American College of Veterinary Behaviorists (ACVB) (www.dacvb.org) and are licensed to diagnose and treat both medical and behavioral canine problems. In addition, a veterinary behaviorist can prescribe medications that may help deal with your Lab's issues.

Certification in behavior counseling is offered by several additional organizations. You can visit their Internet sites to search for a qualified professional to help you with your dog: the Association of Animal Behavior Professionals (AABP) (www.associationofanimalbehaviorprofessionals.com) and the Association of Companion Animal Behavior Counselors (http://animalbehaviorcounselors.org).

# CHAPTER 9

# ACTIVITIES WITH YOUR LABRADOR RETRIEVER

It doesn't matter if you are a man or woman, child or senior, active or couch potato, or even if you have a physical disability—there's an activity for you and your Labrador Retriever. You don't have to be a great athlete to participate, and you aren't required to compete for ribbons and titles. At the same time, if you are an avid competitor, you'll find that canine sports are rewarding and challenging, and you've picked the perfect breed to train.

## PERFORMANCE SPORTS

Performance dog sports include competitive events and other activities in which you can win awards and titles. Many sports award titles for qualifying scores; you don't have to "win," which means that you can participate and achieve high rankings without being a cutthroat competitor if that's not your style. Many of the sports described in this section are American Kennel Club (AKC) activities. The United Kennel Club (UKC) and other organizations offer similar events, although the requirements for each group may differ somewhat.

### AGILITY

Agility requires the dog to run through an obstacle course: jumping, weaving through poles, walking over a teeter-totter and an A-frame. He must do all this within a time limit while remaining under the handler's control and without knocking over an obstacle or causing a "fault," like knocking down a jump. Numerous agility organizations hold events throughout the United States, and each of their competition requirements is slightly different. Agility classes are an exciting way to have fun and exercise your Labrador.

Canine freestyle is a wonderful way to get some exercise and have fun with your dog.

### CANINE FREESTYLE

You don't have to be a great dancer to partner with your own Labrador star and hit the dance

A conformation show evaluates how well a dog conforms to the standard for the breed.

floor. Musical freestyle takes several forms: heeling and obedience moves to musical accompaniment or dance moves choreographed with your dog. Dancers and their dogs develop teamwork, choreography, and interpretation in this canine version of dressage. For more information, visit the World Canine Freestyle Organization, Inc., (WCFO) at www.worldcaninefreestyle.org.

## CONFORMATION

When you hear the term "dog show," you might picture, for example, the annual Westminster Kennel Club dog show. The purpose of conformation shows is to evaluate breeding stock; therefore, only registered intact dogs and bitches can be shown. Dogs are entered in various classes specified by breed, sex, age, and other factors. They are judged as to how well each "conforms" to the breed standard, and the best dogs in each class win ribbons and move up to the final class, where Best of Breed is chosen. In all-breed shows, the Best of Breed Labrador then competes in the Sporting Group against other sporting breeds like Irish Setters, Springer Spaniels, and Pointers. Finally, the Group winner competes against other Group winners for Best in Show. Labrador Retriever breed clubs also hold specialty shows, which are conformation shows in which only Labs compete.

## CONFORMATION CERTIFICATE

The Labrador Retriever Club, Inc., (LRC) the parent club for the breed in the United States, offers a Conformation Certificate. This is an opportunity for owners to have their dogs evaluated and recognized as having basic Labrador Retriever characteristics. The certificate is awarded to any Labrador (even spayed and neutered) over one year of age who passes an examination officiated by an approved judge. The judge considers the following questions:

• Does the dog possess the basic attributes of a Labrador Retriever?
• Does the dog exhibit a majority of breed characteristics?
• Would the dog be excused from a conformation ring due to lack of merit?
• Does the dog possess any disqualifying characteristics?

If you are interested in conformation showing, this certificate is a good place to start. Ask your breeder if your dog has the physical characteristics to do well in the ring. If yes, join a Labrador club, take some handling classes, and make friends with other Lab enthusiasts who will mentor and advise you as you begin your show career. Breed clubs also hold matches where you can practice with your Lab.

If your dog isn't show quality, don't be disappointed; even the smallest fault (such as being too tall or having crooked teeth) may keep him out of the show ring, but it doesn't disqualify him from other types of competition.

## DOCK DIVING

Dock diving is a family event that anyone with a dog and a ball can enjoy. Simply put, the dog who jumps the farthest off a dock into the water wins. There are divisions for Big Air, Extreme Vertical, and Speed Retrieve. Events take place all over the world. It doesn't take a lot of time and training, just an enthusiastic dog who is over six months old. For information on how to get started, visit www.dockdogs.com.

## FIELD TRIALS

Field trials are the oldest competition sport for Labradors, begun back

**BE AWARE!**

If your Lab is not registered but is a purebred, he can get an American Kennel Club PAL/ILP (Purebred Alternative Listing, formerly called Indefinite Listing Privilege) by applying to the AKC. This will make him eligible to compete in all performance events except conformation. All PAL dogs are required to be spayed or neutered. Also, dogs who were purchased with a limited registration are eligible for performance events.

in the 1920s and 30s by wealthy hunters who wanted to compete against each other and show off their dogs' skills. For the dedicated sportsperson and professional trainer, today's field trials feature some of the most skilled handlers and dogs in the U.S. The dog retrieves birds from 200 to 300 yards (183 to 274.5 m) away, at the direction of his handler, and thus earns points toward a championship. The ultimate test of retrieving skills, the highest-scoring dogs achieve the Field Champion (FC) or Amateur Field Champion (AFC) titles. There are also field trial events for young dogs, six months to two years old, who can earn their Derby Championship. Clubs offer more than 250 AKC Retriever field trials in the United States every year.

Field trials are the oldest competition sport for Labs.

## FLYBALL

Flyball is the perfect sport for an active dog with endless energy. Two teams of four dogs each run a relay race over a series of hurdles to the end of a 51-foot (15.5-m) course. At the end, the dog triggers a box that releases a tennis ball, and he brings it back over the jumps to the handler. Then the next dog goes. Assorted breeds or just one breed can run together as a team. The jump heights are determined by the height of the smallest dog on the team, so you'll often see teams with one small and three big dogs. This is an exciting sport, and hundreds of tournaments are held all over the United States every year. Learn more at www.flyball.org.

## HUNTING TESTS

In this sport, a pet owner interested in training a dog for the field, even if not interested in actual hunting, has the opportunity to participate and earn

Hunting tests challenge a Lab to perform the work he was bred to do.

titles. The AKC developed the tests in the early 1980s by forming the North American Hunting Retriever Association (NAHRA). Today the groups have separated, but both still conduct similar events across the country. Almost 400 AKC Retriever Hunting Tests are held in the United States each year, so there are plenty of opportunities to participate.

In AKC tests at the junior level, a dog must complete four single marked retrieves on land and water. The dog sees a bird fall, visually "marks" its location, and retrieves it when released by the handler. He then brings the bird back "to hand" without dropping it. He releases the bird on command, and his soft mouth should not have damaged the bird. When the dog passes four tests, he is awarded the Junior Hunter (JH) title. Handlers don't have to shoot birds—there are throwers out in the field who toss the birds so that they land consistently for each competitor. After the JH title, dogs and handlers can then move up to Senior Hunter (SH) and Master Hunter (MH) tests, which involve "blind" retrieves, where the dog doesn't see the bird fall, and the handler must guide him by signals to find and retrieve it. Advanced tests also include "doubles" and "triples" in which the dog marks multiple falls and must remember where they are and retrieve them in sequence. Dogs also learn to "honor" by sitting quietly while another dog retrieves.

## OBEDIENCE

Obedience competitions demonstrate your dog's training and ability to function as a well-behaved family companion. In an obedience trial, a handler/dog team that earns a score of 170 points out of 200 earns a "leg" toward a title, which requires three qualifying scores under two different judges. You begin in the Novice class and your dog earns the Companion Dog (CD) title, then move up to Open (Companion Dog Excellent, or CDX) and Utility (Utility Dog, or UD). Once you've finished these levels, you can continue competing and earn a Utility Dog Excellent (UDX) or the ultimate title, Obedience Trial Champion (OTCH).

The Novice exercises include heeling both on leash and off, recall, return to *heel* position ("finish"), stand for examination by the judge, a one-minute *sit*, and a three-minute *down*, all in response to the judge's commands. As you enter advanced classes, the exercises get more difficult, and include a three-minute *stay* with the handler out of sight, retrieve a dumbbell and a glove, retrieve over a jump, and respond to hand signals. Dogs are judged on their precision and compliance with the handler's commands.

Some trials offer a Beginner Novice class. Although it is considered a non-regular class and not offered at every trial, it offers beginners a less competitive way to try out obedience. Once your Lab qualifies in three trials from at least two different judges, he earns the Beginner Novice (BN) title. Exercises are performed on leash and are less difficult than in the Novice class.

## RALLY OBEDIENCE

Rally obedience is less structured than obedience trials and is a great place to start your obedience career or just have fun training and showing your Lab. Handler and dog move through a course of 10 to 20 stations at their own pace and perform an obedience exercise at each. The judges look for teamwork more than precision handling. You can talk to and encourage your dog, and he doesn't have to stay in perfect position at all times.

Tasks include commands such as *sit*, *down*, about turn, left turn, and return to *heel* position ("finish"). There are three levels in rally: Novice, Advanced, and Excellent. You can earn a title by getting three qualifying scores of at least 70 out of 100 points from two different judges. Once you have completed all three levels, you can continue to compete and earn the Rally Advanced Excellent (RAE) title.

## TRACKING

Tracking is the perfect sport for Labs, who have an excellent sense of smell. The dog wears a harness while following a human scent track and finds a glove at the end. Dogs can earn several types of tracking titles, each one more advanced. At the beginning level, the dog follows a 440- to 500-yard (402- to 457-m) track that includes several changes of direction. Upon successful completion, he earns his Tracking Dog (TD) title. As dogs move up to the next level (Tracking Dog Excellent, or TDX), the track is older, longer, and becomes more difficult. Variable surface tracking (VST) tests a dog's ability to track in an urban setting. A dog who completes all three tests earns the Champion Tracker (CT) title. Unlike agility and obedience, which require a dog to qualify three times, he only needs to complete one track successfully to earn each title.

During a rally exercise, the handler and dog move through a course of 10 to 20 stations at their own pace and perform an obedience exercise at each.

The best way to get involved in tracking is to find a club or class and train with other people who can lay tracks for you and teach you how to "read" your dog's actions as he tracks.

## WORKING CERTIFICATE

The LRC offers a Working Certificate, similar to the Conformation Certificate, in that it is an entry-level evaluation. It tests the natural retrieving instinct of your dog. To receive a certificate, the dog must demonstrate that he is not gun shy and can retrieve a shot bird at 50 yards (45.7 m) on land. He must then complete two water retrieves to demonstrate that he is willing to enter and re-enter the water. This is a one-time test and is an excellent way to see if you enjoy training and working your dog in the field. The LRC requires that all

Labs who have achieved their conformation championship must also have a Working Certificate before they can use the champion title.

## NONCOMPETITIVE ACTIVITIES FOR YOU AND YOUR LAB

In addition to competitive events and the hours of training you must invest to achieve a title, Labs and their owners can enjoy many other recreational and service activities.

### CANINE GOOD CITIZEN® (CGC) PROGRAM

The AKC's Canine Good Citizen program was instituted to promote well-behaved dogs and responsible owners. The CGC is open to all dogs, registered with the AKC or not. Kennel clubs, dog obedience clubs, dog trainers, and other dog groups often host the training and testing for the CGC.

A dog must successfully complete ten exercises to earn the CGC certificate:
1. accept a stranger stopping to talk with you
2. sit still and accept petting by a stranger

Because Labs are so sociable, dog parks are a great place for them to make friends and get some exercise.

3. allow someone to handle him as a groomer or veterinarian would
4. walk nicely on a loose leash
5. walk nicely through a crowd
6. sit and lie down on command and stay in position as you walk away
7. come when called
8. remain calm in the presence of another dog
9. react confidently in the presence of distractions
10. accept being left alone with someone else without becoming overly anxious

### DOG PARKS

Many communities have a local park set aside just for dogs. Because Labs are so sociable, this is a great place for yours to make friends and get some exercise. A good dog park should be fenced and have separate areas for small and large dogs. A park is only as good as the dogs and owners who visit it. If there are aggressive dogs or owners who do not control their dogs when play gets out of hand, leave. You alone are responsible for your Lab's safety. Responsible dog park visitors clean up after their dogs and monitor their dog's behavior so that no one gets hurt.

## LABRADOR RETRIEVER GET-TOGETHERS

There are Lab lovers' get-togethers all over the United States. Some are yearly, monthly, or even weekly. Owners meet at parks, beaches, and trails with their dogs to share activities and have fun with their dogs. For example, an Internet search for "Labrador Retrievers" at www.meetup.com returned more than 225 members in San Diego County. If there isn't a group near you, you can start one.

## LABRADOR RETRIEVER RESCUE

You may already have your Labrador, but there are many wonderful dogs in need of homes. Rescue volunteers transport dogs, do home visits, screen adopters, make phone calls, staff booths at adoption events, provide foster homes, and get involved in public education. Members bring their own dogs to social events and public outreach.

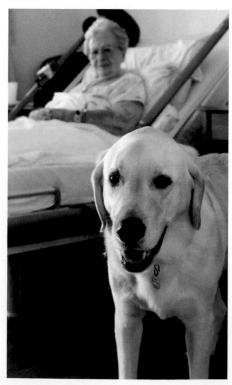

## THERAPY DOGS

Therapy dogs go with their owners to visit people in nursing homes, hospitals, day care centers, schools, and libraries to share friendship with the people they visit. Besides social visits, you and your dog can learn to assist therapists and doctors in actual therapy and rehabilitation sessions.

Most therapy dog organizations require the dog to pass the

Therapy dogs go with their owners to visit people in nursing homes, hospitals, day care centers, schools, and libraries to share friendship with the people they visit.

AKC CGC test prior to certification, but that isn't the only training you and your Labrador must complete. The dog needs to get used to wheelchairs and walkers, canes and crutches—all of the sights, sounds, and smells he'll encounter during visits.

Therapy Dogs International (www.tdi-dog.org) and the Delta Society (www.deltasociety.org) are national organizations with local chapters that train and certify animal-assisted therapy dogs. Many dog trainers offer classes in which you and your dog can learn the necessary skills. The Delta Society also offers a home study course to prepare you and your dog for visits.

## SEARCH AND RESCUE

If your dog really excels at tracking, you can volunteer for search and rescue. This demanding activity gives back to the community while you train your Lab to a higher level. Dogs who do well in search and rescue are extremely focused and can block out distractions like children, other dogs, and interesting smells not related to their search. Searches are always conducted under the direction of local law enforcement agencies.

## ACTIVITIES FOR CHILDREN

There are quite a few activities in which your child and Labrador Retriever can participate.

### 4H

4H (www.4-h.org) is an organization run by your state extension service that offers children from 5 to 19 hands-on learning to develop life skills, including clubs that give kids the opportunity to train and show their dogs (and other pets). Kids get to spend time with their dogs and their friends in a relaxed environment that is not as competitive as AKC events. Many kids exhibit their animals at county and state fairs.

## Dog Tale

Edith Bryan has trained four of her black Labs—Annie, Tess, Meg, and Amber—in search and rescue, and they volunteer regularly near her home. Her dogs have participated in more than 40 successful searches over the past seven years. Typically they are called out to find lost children or adults in local wooded areas and rural neighborhoods. Search calls can come any time, night or day, and they must be ready to head out at a moment's notice.

## AKC JUNIOR SHOWMANSHIP

For children who think they want to show dogs, maybe even professionally, AKC Junior Showmanship offers kids from ages 9 to 18 a chance to learn and compete in the world of purebred dogs. Even if they don't pursue the sport professionally, showing dogs is a hobby they can enjoy all their lives (www.akc.org/kids_juniors/jr_getting_started.cfm).

## BOY/GIRL SCOUTS

Both the Boy Scouts and Girl Scouts offer pet care achievement badges. In the Boy Scouts (www.scouting.org), it is the Dog Care merit badge. Brownie Girl Scouts (www.girlscouts.org) participate in the Animal Care "Try-It", and Junior Girl Scouts can earn the Pet Care badge. For dog-loving children, this is a great way to get them involved with dogs in a structured way.

## TRAVELING WITH LABBY

With a little planning, your Lab can join you on family vacations, especially if your plans include outdoor activities. Before you decide to take Labby along, ensure that he will be safe and happy wherever you go.

The following are some essential travel tips:
- An interstate health certificate from your veterinarian is required when crossing state lines. Requirements vary by state.
- If your dog is not currently on heartworm preventive, he may need it if you are traveling to areas of the U.S. where it is common.
- Get a new ID tag with your cell phone number on it. Then, if your Lab gets lost, people can contact you quickly; there's no point in calling your house if you're not there. Carry his microchip number and license information with you.

- Check ahead to see if the campgrounds, hotels, and parks you plan to visit allow dogs and if there are any restrictions. For example, national parks allow dogs on leash but don't allow them on every trail.
- Bring your Lab's food, or be sure that the same brand is available where you are going. You don't want to have to change brands in the middle of a trip. Traveling disrupts a dog's routine and digestion; you don't want to compound the upset by switching his food too.
- Bring clean-up supplies: poop bags, scooper, and odor neutralizer. Be a good citizen, and pick up after your dog everywhere you go. Leaving dog piles in public areas is just plain rude. Your dog's feces could carry parasites or seeds from non-native plants, which can invade and destroy natural habitats.
- If you can, bring your Lab's bed or favorite toy from home. Traveling is stressful for dogs, and the smell of familiar things will help him settle in when you reach your destination.

Traveling with your dog on vacation can be a great adventure for both of you.

- Keep your Lab on leash! Rest areas and hotel parking lots are not good places to let him wander. Even a mellow Lab will be uncertain in a new place and could easily spook and run off. You also don't want him to run up to strangers, especially children. Even if they love dogs, a strange dog rushing at them is frightening.

## TRAVELING BY CAR

If traveling by car, buckle up for safety. This warning applies to people *and* dogs. Your own safety is at risk when there's a loose dog in the car; you don't need a big otter tail whacking you in the face as he jumps into the backseat. Also, the kids and dog are all more likely to settle down and behave if everyone is strapped in. If you are in an accident, your Lab could be injured or thrown from the car and lost if he is not restrained. The best plan is to keep him in a crate while you are driving. If that's not possible, canine seat belts are available, or you can fashion your own from a walking harness.

Some additional tips include:

- Bring medication in case your Lab gets carsick. A dog may be fine riding around town, but winding mountain roads can upset his stomach as easily as yours.
- Carry water from home, and stop every two or three hours for a canine potty break and big drink of water.
- A crate covered with luggage in the back corner of a van can get too hot, and your dog will quickly become dehydrated and overheated. Protect his crate from direct sunlight and make sure that he gets plenty of fresh air.

## TRAVELING BY AIR

Airlines require you to supply a hard plastic crate for your Lab. Each airline has specific requirements; usually the crate needs to be big enough for your dog to stand up and turn around. Write your name, phone number, and destination

**BE AWARE!**

If you are traveling in the heat of summer, don't leave your Lab in the car while you go to an amusement park or restaurant. In just minutes, extreme heat can build up in a closed vehicle and can kill a pet. When I moved from Seattle to San Diego, I drove south during the blistering heat of early July with four dogs crated in my van. When I stopped at rest areas, I walked all four dogs into the large handicapped access bathroom stall with me because it was too hot to leave them in the car.

address on the crate with a felt pen. All airlines require a health certificate, usually issued within the last ten days, and proof of rabies vaccine.

The American Veterinary Medical Association (AVMA) does not recommend tranquilizers for flying. Sedatives can cause respiratory problems when combined with pressure from the high altitude. A sedated dog will also lose his balance when the crate is moved. Discuss this option with your veterinarian if you think that a tranquilizer is necessary, and note the name of the drug, dosage, and time administered on the crate so that airline personnel are aware of it.

Reserve a nonstop flight if at all possible. Your dog could get moved to the wrong plane or overheated in the cargo hold during a plane change or layover. In the summer, try to fly at night when temperatures are lower. A crate sitting out on the hot tarmac is a death trap. Many airlines will not fly animals at temperatures under 35°F (2°C) or over 85°F (30°C).

## PET-FRIENDLY LODGING

Many hotels, RV parks, and campgrounds throughout the United States allow dogs. Check in advance, though, to be sure that they allow large dogs. Some will charge an extra nightly fee for your pet. Many hotels will provide doggy day care while you are out sightseeing during the day. Some offer additional amenities, from special treats to fancy dog beds and bowls. Make reservations ahead of time because some facilities set aside a limited number of rooms or sites for dog owners.

As you can see, there are endless fun opportunities for you and your Labrador Retriever. My wish for you is many years of fun and friendship with America's—and my—favorite breed.

# RESOURCES

## ASSOCIATIONS AND ORGANIZATIONS

### BREED CLUBS

**American Kennel Club (AKC)**
5580 Centerview Drive
Raleigh, NC 27606
Telephone: (919) 233-9767
Fax: (919) 233-3627
E-Mail: info@akc.org
www.akc.org

**Canadian Kennel Club (CKC)**
89 Skyway Avenue, Suite 100
Etobicoke, Ontario M9W 6R4
Telephone: (416) 675-5511
Fax: (416) 675-6506
E-Mail: information@ckc.ca
www.ckc.ca

**Federation Cynologique Internationale (FCI)**
Secretariat General de la FCI
Place Albert 1er, 13
B – 6530 Thuin
Belqique
www.fci.be

**The Kennel Club**
1 Clarges Street
London
W1J 8AB
Telephone: 0870 606 6750
Fax: 0207 518 1058
www.the-kennel-club.org.uk

**The Labrador Retriever Club, Inc.**
www.thelabradorclub.com

**Labrador Retriever Club of Canada**
www.labradorretrieverclub.ca

**The Labrador Retriever Club of Great Britain**
www.thelabradorretrieverclub.com

**United Kennel Club (UKC)**
100 E. Kilgore Road
Kalamazoo, MI 49002-5584
Telephone: (269) 343-9020
Fax: (269) 343-7037
E-Mail: pbickell@ukcdogs.com
www.ukcdogs.com

## PET SITTERS

**National Association of Professional Pet Sitters**
15000 Commerce Parkway, Suite C
Mt. Laurel, New Jersey 08054
Telephone: (856) 439-0324
Fax: (856) 439-0525
E-Mail: napps@ahint.com
www.petsitters.org

**Pet Sitters International**
201 East King Street
King, NC 27021-9161
Telephone: (336) 983-9222
Fax: (336) 983-5266
E-Mail: info@petsit.com
www.petsit.com

## RESCUE ORGANIZATIONS AND ANIMAL WELFARE GROUPS

**American Humane Association (AHA)**
63 Inverness Drive East
Englewood, CO 80112
Telephone: (303) 792-9900
Fax: 792-5333
www.americanhumane.org

**American Society for the Prevention of Cruelty to Animals (ASPCA)**
424 E. 92nd Street
New York, NY 10128-6804
Telephone: (212) 876-7700
www.aspca.org

**The Humane Society of the United States (HSUS)**
2100 L Street, NW
Washington DC 20037
Telephone: (202) 452-1100
www.hsus.org

**Royal Society for the Prevention of Cruelty to Animals (RSPCA)**
RSPCA Enquiries Service
Wilberforce Way, Southwater,
Horsham, West Sussex RH13 9RS
United Kingdom
Telephone: 0870 3335 999
Fax: 0870 7530 284
www.rspca.org.uk

## SPORTS

**International Agility Link (IAL)**
Global Administrator: Steve Drinkwater
E-Mail: yunde@powerup.au
www.agilityclick.com/~ial

**The World Canine Freestyle Organization, Inc.**
P.O. Box 350122
Brooklyn, NY 11235
Telephone: (718) 332-8336
Fax: (718) 646-2686
E-Mail: WCFODOGS@aol.com
www.worldcaninefreestyle.org

## THERAPY

**Delta Society**
875 124th Ave, NE, Suite 101
Bellevue, WA 98005
Telephone: (425) 679-5500
Fax: (425) 679-5539
E-Mail: info@DeltaSociety.org
www.deltasociety.org

**Therapy Dogs Inc.**
P.O. Box 20227
Cheyenne WY 82003
Telephone: (877) 843-7364
Fax: (307) 638-2079
E-Mail: therapydogsinc@
qwestoffice.net
www.therapydogs.com

**Therapy Dogs International (TDI)**
88 Bartley Road
Flanders, NJ 07836
Telephone: (973) 252-9800
Fax: (973) 252-7171
E-Mail: tdi@gti.net
www.tdi-dog.org

## TRAINING

**Association of Pet Dog Trainers (APDT)**
150 Executive Center Drive Box 35
Greenville, SC 29615
Telephone: (800) PET-DOGS
Fax: (864) 331-0767
E-Mail: information@apdt.com
www.apdt.com

**International Association of Animal Behavior Consultants (IAABC)**
565 Callery Road
Cranberry Township, PA 16066
E-Mail: info@iaabc.org
www.iaabc.org

**National Association of Dog Obedience Instructors (NADOI)**
PMB 369
729 Grapevine Hwy.
Hurst, TX 76054-2085
www.nadoi.org

## VETERINARY AND HEALTH RESOURCES

**Academy of Veterinary Homeopathy (AVH)**
P.O. Box 9280
Wilmington, DE 19809
Telephone: (866) 652-1590
Fax: (866) 652-1590
www.theavh.org

**American Academy of Veterinary Acupuncture (AAVA)**
P.O. Box 1058
Glastonbury, CT 06033
Telephone: (860) 632-9911
Fax: (860) 659-8772
www.aava.org

**American Animal Hospital Association (AAHA)**
12575 W. Bayaud Ave.
Lakewood, CO 80228
Telephone: (303) 986-2800
Fax: (303) 986-1700
E-Mail: info@aahanet.org
www.aahanet.org/index.cfm

**American College of Veterinary Internal Medicine (ACVIM)**
1997 Wadsworth Blvd., Suite A
Lakewood, CO 80214-5293
Telephone: (800) 245-9081
Fax: (303) 231-0880
Email: ACVIM@ACVIM.org
www.acvim.org

**American College of Veterinary Ophthalmologists (ACVO)**
P.O. Box 1311
Meridian, ID 83860
Telephone: (208) 466-7624
Fax: (208) 466-7693
E-Mail: office09@acvo.com
www.acvo.com

**American Holistic Veterinary Medical Association (AHVMA)**
2218 Old Emmorton Road
Bel Air, MD 21015
Telephone: (410) 569-0795
Fax: (410) 569-2346
E-Mail: office@ahvma.org
www.ahvma.org

**American Veterinary Medical Association (AVMA)**
1931 North Meacham Road, Suite 100
Schaumburg, IL 60173-4360
Telephone: (847) 925-8070
Fax: (847) 925-1329
E-Mail: avmainfo@avma.org
www.avma.org

**ASPCA Animal Poison Control Center**
Telephone: (888) 426-4435
www.aspca.org

**British Veterinary Association (BVA)**
7 Mansfield Street
London
W1G 9NQ
Telephone: 0207 636 6541
Fax: 0207 908 6349
E-Mail: bvahq@bva.co.uk
www.bva.co.uk

Canine Eye Registration
Foundation (CERF)
VMDB/CERF
1717 Philo Rd
P O Box 3007
Urbana, IL 61803-3007
Telephone: (217) 693-4800
Fax: (217) 693-4801
E-Mail: CERF@vmbd.org
www.vmdb.org

### Orthopedic Foundation for Animals (OFA)
2300 NE Nifong Blvd
Columbus, Missouri 65201-3856
Telephone: (573) 442-0418
Fax: (573) 875-5073
Email: ofa@offa.org
www.offa.org

### US Food and Drug Administration Center for Veterinary Medicine (CVM)
7519 Standish Place
HFV-12
Rockville, MD 20855-0001
Telephone: (240) 276-9300 or (888) INFO-FDA
http://www.fda.gov/cvm

## PUBLICATIONS
### BOOKS
Anderson, Teoti. *The Super Simple Guide to Housetraining*. Neptune City: TFH Publications, 2004.

Anne, Jonna, with Mary Straus. *The Healthy Dog Cookbook: 50 Nutritious and Delicious Recipes Your Dog Will Love*. UK: Ivy Press Limited, 2008.

Dainty, Suellen. *50 Games to Play With Your Dog*. UK: Ivy Press Limited, 2007.

Morgan, Diane. *The Labrador Retriever*. Neptune City: TFH Publications, Inc. 2005.

Moustaki, Nikki. *Labrador Retrievers*. Neptune City: TFH Publications, Inc. 2006.

Rehkopf, Linda. *Labrador Retriever*. Neptune City: TFH Publications, Inc. 2010.

## MAGAZINES
### AKC Family Dog
American Kennel Club
260 Madison Avenue
New York, NY 10016
Telephone: (800) 490-5675
E-Mail: familydog@akc.org
www.akc.org/pubs/familydog

### AKC Gazette
American Kennel Club
260 Madison Avenue
New York, NY 10016
Telephone: (800) 533-7323
E-Mail: gazette@akc.org
www.akc.org/pubs/gazette

### Dog & Kennel
Pet Publishing, Inc.
7-L Dundas Circle
Greensboro, NC 27407
Telephone: (336) 292-4272
Fax: (336) 292-4272
E-Mail: info@petpublishing.com
www.dogandkennel.com

### Dogs Monthly
Ascot House
High Street, Ascot,
Berkshire SL5 7JG
United Kingdom
Telephone: 0870 730 8433
Fax: 0870 730 8431
E-Mail: admin@rtc-associates.freeserve.co.uk
www.corsini.co.uk/dogsmonthly

## WEBSITES
Nylabone
www.nylabone.com

TFH Publications, Inc.
www.tfh.com

# INDEX

Boldfaced numbers indicate illustrations.

## PHOTO CREDITS

## DEDICATION

This book is dedicated to the memory of my Labrador, Tank, U-CD Tiger Mountain's Yellow Gold, CD, JH, CGC. He was my once-in-a-lifetime dog, and taught me so much.

## ACKNOWLEDGMENTS

Thank you to the many people who helped me in my research for this book, including Edith Bryan, Julie Cantrell, Don and Barbara Ironside, Nina Mann, Angie Meeks, Sarbjit Singh, DVM, and Frances Smith, DVM, PH.D.

## ABOUT THE AUTHOR

**Terry Albert** is an award-winning writer and artist specializing in pet-related subjects. She has had hands-on experience with many breeds of dogs as a

professional dog trainer, foster home provider, and professional pet sitter. She has fostered more than 100 homeless Labradors for rescue groups and was a founding member of Southern California Labrador Retriever Rescue. She also served as public education coordinator for Puget Sound Labrador Retriever Association and was a member of the San Diego Labrador Retriever Club.

In addition, Terry served on the Board of Directors for Seattle Purebred Dog Rescue, the Humane Society of Seattle/King County, and LabMed, which funds medical care for homeless Labs. She also volunteers as a reserve park ranger in the mounted patrol for the city of Poway in Southern California. Terry is also known for her paintings of Labradors, and she designed the annual logo for the Labrador Retriever Club, Inc.'s, (LRC) national specialty show for numerous years. Her artwork of Labs and other breeds has been exhibited at the Art Show at the Dog Show and the American Kennel Club (AKC) Museum of the Dog. She currently works from her home, which she shares with four dogs, four horses, two cats, and two box turtles.

## ABOUT ANIMAL PLANET™

Animal Planet™ is the only television network dedicated exclusively to the connection between humans and animals. The network brings people of all ages together by tapping into our fundamental fascination with animals through an array of fresh programming that includes humor, competition, drama, and spectacle from the animal kingdom.

## ABOUT *DOGS 101*

The most comprehensive—and most endearing—dog encyclopedia on television, *DOGS 101* spotlights the adorable, the feisty and the unexpected. A wide-ranging rundown of everyone's favorite dog breeds—from the Dalmatian to Xoloitzcuintli—this series surveys a variety of breeds for their behavioral quirks, genetic history, most famous examples and wildest trivia. Learn which dogs are best for urban living and which would be the best fit for your family. Using a mix of animal experts, pop-culture footage and stylized dog photography, *DOGS 101* is an unprecedented look at man's best friend.